MONETARY REFORM
FOR THE
WORLD ECONOMY

THE ELIHU ROOT LECTURES

MONETARY REFORM
FOR THE
WORLD ECONOMY

by

ROBERT V. ROOSA

Published for the

COUNCIL ON FOREIGN RELATIONS

by

HARPER & ROW, Publishers

New York and Evanston

The Council on Foreign Relations is a non-profit institution devoted to the study of political, economic, and strategic problems as related to American foreign policy. It takes no stand, expressed or implied, on American policy.

The authors of books published under the auspices of the Council are responsible for their statements of fact and expressions of opinion. The Council is responsible only for determining that they should be presented to the public.

For a list of Council publications see pages 170–173.

IN MEMORY OF EDWARD JOHN NOBLE

The publication of this volume of The Elihu Root Lectures was aided by a grant from the Edward John Noble Foundation in memory of Mr. Noble and his interest in encouraging American leadership.

PREFACE

THE TWENTY YEARS since World War II have seen more creative change and innovation in the monetary arrangements serving the nations of the world than any previous two decades in recorded history. Yet there is still widespread dissatisfaction. Able critics have become alarmed; many of them predict imminent crisis unless major further reforms are initiated at once.

As will become repeatedly apparent to readers of this little volume, I do not share that extreme alarm. But I do think the time has come for reappraisal—in three ways. First, it is important to try to sort out those elements of the international monetary system which seem now, after the experience of these two decades, to warrant a lasting place within the patterns of change that may evolve in the future. Second, it is equally important to sort through the various reasons that have been suggested for reform or change, to discover which are consistent with each other, and to try to find any common area of overlap that may exist between the valid objectives for further change and the elements that must be preserved in the system we already have. Third, having found the common boundaries that describe both the necessary area of continuity and the area for possible change, it is important to identify issues and develop principles within that common ground so that action can be taken, whenever there is a general consensus that the time for further action has come.

These pages are an attempt in this direction. During my period of service in the United States Treasury from 1961 through 1964, I shared in the earliest concerted efforts along these lines that were made by the official representatives of several countries in various forums, efforts that became systematized in 1963 and are still continuing. I have done my best here to avoid drawing upon any of the exchanges which still remain confidential—other than views which have long been my own. But actual authorship is untraceable in subjects as vast as these, and I must acknowledge, without specific attribution or imputation, my own sense of deep obligation not only to all of my former colleagues in the United States government but also to those from other countries and from the various international institutions. Most notably, these are the men whose names accompany the Annex prepared by the Deputies of the Group of Ten, which is included for convenient reference as an appendix to these chapters.

The chapters themselves are substantially as prepared for delivery as The Elihu Root Lectures on May 10, 17, and 24, 1965, in the "off-the-record" atmosphere of the Council on Foreign Relations. Only parts of each were actually used in the oral presentation; but all have profited from the criticisms aroused there. I am especially grateful also for critical reading of the manuscript by Douglas Dillon; Pierre-Paul Schweitzer and Frank Southard of the International Monetary Fund and by the United States Executive Director, William Dale; Frederick L. Deming, Merlyn Trued, and George Willis of the United States Treasury; Benjamin Caplan of the Department of State; William McChesney Martin, J. Dewey Daane, and Ralph A. Young of the Board of Governors of the Federal Reserve System; Alan Holmes of the Federal Reserve Bank of New York; and my earliest collaborator in writing on monetary affairs, Peter L. Bernstein.

For the final processing of all that follows I am heavily indebted to the splendid staff of the Council itself, particularly to Robert Valkenier the Council's able editor, and to my indefatigable secretary, Mrs. Charles Dorsey, as well as to my partners at Brown Brothers Harriman & Co. No one mentioned or unmentioned has had any responsibility at any stage, however, for what is said. That burden is all mine. My wife, though also blameless as to the views, or the errors, deserves all credit for this effort having reached completion.

R. V. R.

June 11, 1965

CONTENTS

I

THE CONDITIONS FOR MONETARY ORDER

Introduction

Eₗᵢₕᵤ ᵣₒₒₜ lives in the traditions of world diplomacy as one of its greatest spokesmen for systematic, but pragmatic, international cooperation among sovereign nations. For him, international order began with the maintenance of conditions in which each nation-state could flourish. Each should have its own constellation of bilateral agreements with others. These constellations would inevitably become intermingled. New and more embracing agreements among groups of nations could then emerge, from experience already gained. And in time, a body of universally respected law would take shape—relying perhaps on various supranational bodies for its interpretation and its implementation, but relying for its authority on the responsibility of the individual participating nations.

There is a just coincidence in attempting to review the evolution of the international monetary system in a lecture series dedicated to the achievements of Elihu Root and to his memory. For that system has itself evolved in a manner that he would, I believe, understand and commend. To begin with, it is not, in the strict sense that would satisfy a scientist, a system at all. It is an array of institutions and procedures, originating in the conditions of each of the one hundred fifty or more individual nation-states in the world today and functioning on the basis of various checks and balances among them. A variety of interlaced networks of treaties and agreements between and among these countries helps to hold the system, such as it is, together and to provide a pattern of conventionally acceptable arrangements for making the payments that are needed for the flow of goods and capital throughout the world.

The most significant unifying influence of modern times upon this international monetary system has been provided through the partial codification of principles and procedures, and also objectives, in the Charter of the International Monetary Fund (IMF) in 1944. The IMF itself, while possessing little coercive power that would impinge on national sovereignty, does receive from the monetary authorities of all its member countries (presently 102) a contribution out of their own monetary reserves, as well as a contribution of their own currency. These, under conditions agreed upon by the members, it can in turn lend to the central banks or governments of particular members.

Beneath the level of the IMF, there are any number of special relations among groups of countries, or between one country and several of its trading partners, concerning the terms on which trade or payments may be conducted or on which monetary reserves may be borrowed or loaned. Each country has, in turn, sole responsibility for the issuance and control of its own currency at home, although the way in which that currency will be made available in exchange for other currencies to settle the country's accounts with the rest of the world must conform to the International Monetary Fund's rules in the case of member countries. The actual financing of specific transactions by the individuals or concerns within each country is, of course, handled by the domestic banking facilities of that country.

This is a tier of national responsibilities, building toward a functioning framework of international arrangements, that Elihu Root would, I suspect, have found quite normal, indeed quite promising, in fulfilling the pattern of progress toward world order that he sought. Nor would he have been surprised, nor discouraged, to hear at intervals a swelling chorus of impatience sounding loudly in complaint because in this, as in other areas of international relations, the system was said to be in danger of breaking down—failing to meet the advancing needs of a dynamic world society. For it is often at such periods of converging complaints, coming from many sides, that nations undertake the re-examination which an evolving, heterogeneous system needs from time to time in order to renew its strengths, repair its weaknesses, and explore new possibilities for the future. And it is far better to be prepared in that way for the possible than to be left to improvise amid the disorder of the unanticipated.

That is why the subject of these lectures has a certain timeliness in 1965. For since the end of 1958, when a number of the leading countries (for the first time in over two decades) made their own currencies convertible with others at fixed rates of exchange (or parities), a series of financial "near-crises" has occurred. The pound sterling and the dollar have for various and different reasons been under intermittent strain in the foreign-exchange markets of the world; the economies of several European countries have suffered inflationary distortions, also for a variety of different reasons; and, partly because of these disturbances, the heads of state of a number of countries, large and small, not to mention a host of scholars and other critics, have proclaimed their grave concern that the supply of world liquidity was too scarce—or too abundant—or too uncertain.

To be sure, over these same years, the volume of world trade has increased proportionately and absolutely by much more than in any comparable peacetime period; the aggregate growth of the gross product of all nations has also set new records; and a remarkable profusion of innovations has been introduced into the bilateral and multilateral financial arrangements of the international monetary system—a system quite capable of servicing the growing dimensions of trade and payments and of meeting the various pressures that have occurred. Thus far, despite the alarms and what may have been some near-misses, it would seem that the system has served the world well. There has been adequate liquidity in the form of the currencies used for making payments on a world-wide scale, the credit facilities needed to finance trade, and the reserves or credits drawn upon by governments to meet over-all shortages in their national accounts with other countries. There may be some significance, indeed, in the fact that complaints of too little liquidity have been about as frequent as those suggesting there has been too much. The argument could even be made, moreover, that in reaching these reasonably balanced results the monetary system has accomplished more toward the stimulation of effective international cooperation over these years than have the various military or diplomatic alliances or arrangements.

Yet not even a record of achievement should of itself silence the critics. Perhaps there is much more that the system could have done, without impairing what it has accomplished. Or perhaps these recent gains have been the supreme final effort of a system that has been eroding underneath. Or perhaps the problems sensed by the critics are those to be expected from new influences, not yet experienced but likely to occur, such as the drying-up of the supply of new dollars in the world that would take place with a continuation of the surplus being achieved during the spring of 1965 in the United States balance of payments. Or perhaps the problem is, more broadly, that the world has been fortunate to have thus far obtained sufficient liquidity from sources that are by their nature unstable, irregular, or haphazard—that the need, if there is to be reliable provision of the liquidity to support sustained economic progress in the future, is for the addition of some other element or component to help regularize and assure an appropriate over-all growth of liquidity for the international monetary system over the decades ahead.

These are the kinds of questions that have prompted the reappraisal attempted here. In this first chapter, with a brevity that forbids digression into historical origins, the effort will be to identify those many features of the existing international monetary system which have become fundamental—the premises on which any future changes must, at least in this writer's view, be firmly rested. In the next, the various objectives that have been proposed for further monetary reform will be evaluated in terms of their consistency with the essentials of the system on which the world depends today. Is there, within the scope permitted by the essential continuing elements of the system, any room for the changes implied by some of the various proposals for reform? Is there, or can there be, common ground shared by the old system and the proposals for the new, within which more can be done to cultivate productive change for the future? The concluding chapter will suggest that there are some promising possibilities for future development, as this becomes necessary, within a system which preserves the needed elements that have evolved out of past experience.

In turning to the appraisal of the system as it has evolved thus far, I have found a four-part approach most useful. First, I think we have to try to discover what is meant by monetary order in the world today, or at the least to take careful note of some of the characteristics or ingredients of monetary order. For without an environment of order and confidence in the monetary system, as a prerequisite, not very much can be done to encourage the trade upon which an expanding world economy depends. Second, I shall merely enumerate, without elaboration, a number of propositions or premises that seem to me virtually incontrovertible in describing the functioning of the international monetary system for as far ahead as any foreseeable future may extend. Third, I think a more intensive search may be useful into several conditions that seem to me to be essential for monetary order in the world, but which are certainly controversial and will require supporting argument if the reader is to accompany me into the later analysis. And finally, I think mention should be made of some of the steps forward that have been taken in international financial cooperation during recent years—steps that can have a great potential for further development within the international monetary system, whatever may come of the various reform proposals to be discussed in subsequent chapters.

The Meaning of Monetary Order

An orderly system of world payments requires the effective operation, in some unison, of three sets of functions: (1) those within each country that provide its own currency for its own use; (2) those available to the banks and traders of each country to provide a vehicle currency (a "world trading currency") for use in making payments to the banks and traders of other countries; and (3) those available to the monetary authorities of each country to provide reserves that can be used for purchasing its own currency in the foreign-exchange markets or making payments to the monetary authorities of other countries. National or domestic currencies, vehicle or trading currencies for everyday use abroad, and reserve assets (including gold, reserve currencies, and claims on the IMF)—these are the three crucial segments of the system as a whole.

It must be taken as a fact of life now, regardless of the extent to which gold may be used within any of these three segments, that each will also consist in some part of created money. In practice, gold is used very little for either domestic circulation or payments among the banks and traders of the world. Ordinarily, in today's conditions most countries use their own currencies almost exclusively for their own domestic needs, and these currencies are all created by their own central banks and their own commercial banking systems.

For use as a vehicle in ordinary foreign transactions, any widely known and generally acceptable national currency can be employed. So far as the credit needed to finance foreign trade is concerned, some part of that is supplied by the commercial banking systems of virtually all countries. But so far as the currencies actually used in payment are concerned, simple convenience and a desire for uniformity in invoicing and in making payments have caused most of the banks and traders of the world to concentrate their transactions in a few leading currencies. As a result, the bulk of all transactions in international trade is in practice actually carried out primarily in pounds sterling or dollars. The operating or transactions balances which banks and traders have to maintain in readily available liquid form are consequently held mainly in those two currencies, with much the larger part in dollars. In turn, partly as a by-product, a rather large part of the financing of trade credit throughout the world is done by British and American banks.

For reserve purposes, countries prefer to hold an asset that comes as close as possible to being universally acceptable. That is why gold has for centuries been the principal reserve asset and has been the center of doctrinal preoccupation in writings on money from the earliest civilizations down through the mercantilists to the modern day. Any other reserve asset, such as a claim on the IMF or a national currency held in the reserves of another country, must in turn come as close as possible to being "as good as gold." As the international monetary system followed the domestic systems of individual countries in seeking to economize on the uses of gold, reserve currencies have gained a special acceptability because they could, or to the extent that they could, be readily invested or borrowed at short term in their own markets, be serviced by extensive capital markets, and be convertible on demand into gold or something recognized as equivalent to gold.

Subject to some limitations, the pound still fulfills a reserve function for much of the sterling area, and in part for a number of other countries; the French franc has filled a comparable role for many of the present or former French overseas territories; but at least since World War II most of the growth in reserve needs, apart from that met by gold, has been provided by increased holdings of dollars. For the dollar, in addition to fulfilling the conditions just mentioned for a reserve currency somewhat more fully than any alternative currency, has also been much more nearly stable in purchasing power over the past twenty years, and particularly for the past seven or eight years. Moreover, the political stability and enormous economic and military strength of the United States have also increased the desirability—both for official holders and for unofficial holders—

of keeping balances here rather than in any other country in the world.

In the system as it has evolved, gold has become a pillar of stability, while reserve currencies and credit facilities have been built around it to carry the bulk of the regular burdens of fulfilling the reserve needs of individual countries. Nations, just as individuals, need growing supplies of cash or of credit facilities to meet the shortfalls or absorb the overages in their accounts with the rest of the world as trade expands. More recently, greater attention has centered, too, on the way in which the IMF provides additional reserves to the countries whose currencies are used by the IMF in meeting the drawings of other members. In 1964 and 1965, for example, several countries experienced significant increases in their reserves as the counterpart of the use of their currencies by the IMF in meeting large United Kingdom drawings.

Inevitably, in a system which depends—in all three of its segments—upon a variable supply of created money, there will be recurrent collisions between the role of that money as a medium of exchange and its role as a standard of value. As a medium of exchange, money must be expansible to serve the needs of growing trade, and one innovation has followed another over the years in order to fulfill that objective. As a standard of value, however, money must be limited in quantity in order to conserve its purchasing power for those who hold it over the years. The risk has always been that methods of creating money, once learned, would be abused through excessive expansion as the "needs of trade" led to spiralling over-issue. And the subsequent risk has been that over-issue would be followed by constriction, sometimes of a cumulative sort, as the same methods were reversed.

The conditions for monetary order, ultimately, are those which assure that the management of money creation in all three segments of the international system—that is, the management of the national, the vehicle, and the reserve currencies—will year by year allow an addition to the total supply of money that is, to put it somewhat less than profoundly, "just enough and not too much." Naïve though the truism may sound, it bears repeating that the medium of exchange must be fully adequate for all of the real transactions that can reasonably be expected to flow; but the quantity of money, in relation to the various facilities affecting its rate of use, must not increase so rapidly as to depreciate its acceptability as a standard and store of value.

For monetary order there must also be a ready interconvertibility among the moneys used in the three segments of the system, subject of course to the limits set by some countries through exchange controls. And it is, in turn, the discipline of maintaining the convertibility of their own currencies into the vehicle and reserve currencies that impels most countries to try to achieve balance or surplus in their international accounts. Moreover, to the extent that each can maintain balance, achieving adjustment with a minimum of swings in either external surpluses or deficits, its needs for official reserves of liquidity are reduced. There is, therefore, a very close connection between the potential scale of any world-wide need for monetary reserves and the effectiveness of the processes of balance-of-payments adjustment that countries are prepared to pursue. The speedier the adjustment, the smaller the need for reserves (or credit) is likely to be. Analysis of the adjustment process is, consequently, an inherent part of any appraisal of liquidity needs (either for owned reserves or for reserves that may be borrowed).

Not all deficits are necessarily evil, to be sure, nor are all surpluses necessarily disruptive. Most countries have, for long periods, run deficits in the form of imports of long-term capital to establish their productive base adequately and efficiently. And the surpluses of the United States after 1935, for example, were for a long period largely involuntary, resulting from the disarray of political and economic conditions in much of the world, and later enabling the United States to play an unprecedented role in monetary reconstruction after the war.

Problems arise from those deficits which, after taking all the routine trade and capital movements into account, still leave a financing gap which cannot be closed without continuing heavy use of reserves, or special extraordinary borrowing, or both. In effect, these are deficits that in the end place a forced draft on the resources of other countries. The surpluses that create problems are those produced by maintaining particular restrictions on trade or capital flows: surpluses that result in a sustained absorption of reserves, burdening the supply of international liquidity with what is a virtual hoarding demand, denying potential markets to deficit countries capable of earning their own way, and perpetuating an irreconcilable imbalance within the structure of world trade and payments. It is imbalances of this nature, whether on the deficit or the surplus side, that should be corrected if the world economy is to achieve the general conditions of stability, indeed of monetary order, that encourage optimum growth.

There is still one more dimension of monetary order that should be mentioned. The adjustment of imbalance, when it occurs, should be brought about smoothly. No one country should expect, for example, simply to transfer its deficit abruptly to another country or countries, whether these others are currently in surplus or in deficit. The repercussions of abrupt adjustment, moreover, might also result in cumulative retaliation, disrupting rather than restoring order for the monetary system as a whole. That is one of the key reasons why countries need reserves, in order to be able to ride out a corrective readjustment that should be gradual. But an intensely competitive drive for reserves can also have distorting effects. That is one of the principal reasons why, as a supplement to reserves, the availability of credit (sometimes referred to as "conditional liquidity") has become an integral part of the liquidity structure both at the IMF and in various other bilateral and multilateral arrangements. Credit is important for the deficit country in need of funds to finance a gap while working out a satisfactory adjustment so that it can eventually "earn back" the sums to provide for repayment.

Credit is also important, correspondingly, where an orderly correction of a persistent surplus may take time. In those circumstances, there is a useful role for lending by the surplus country of the redundant reserves that it has accumulated.

Monetary order for the international payments system must depend, it appears, upon an effective translation into international terms of the lessons that many countries have learned in domestic terms as they developed the use of money over the past half century or more. There should be some means for flexibly adapting the supply of money, at least in an approximate way, to the reasonably growing needs at reasonably stable prices of the world economy as a whole. There must at the same time be public familiarity with and confidence in the currencies that the public is expected to use. This implies that there should be a ready exchangeability between national currencies and the currencies that serve as vehicles for the transactions of the public in world trade. And there should be a ready substitutability, as well, between these other currencies and all forms of monetary reserves.

These objectives require the maintenance of international conditions that will:

—exert corrective discipline upon individual countries that are in sustained deficit or sustained surplus;
—assure an ample supply of money and credit for the customary transactions among traders and banks throughout the world;
—provide the credit needed to cushion or avert unduly abrupt corrective changes; and
—maintain sufficient monetary reserves (including facilities for lending and borrowing them) to meet the continuing growth of official requirements as trade and payments expand within and among the countries of the world.

Some Established Fundamentals of the System

In striving toward the objectives listed above, the nations of the world have evolved some procedures and principles of a fundamental nature that are now virtually above controversy. Each will be taken for granted in the subsequent chapters. They are listed in the following paragraphs without elaboration.

1. In the ordinary flows of commerce among nations, transactions between buyers and sellers or lenders and borrowers—other than central banks and governments—will be carried out in the currencies of individual countries. That is, goods will be invoiced and credits will be denominated in the kinds of currencies with which private traders and bankers are familiar. In conducting their foreign transactions they will, for the most part, convert their individual national currencies into one of the leading currencies in order to minimize confusion and costs, and to avoid the need for detailed accounting in the currencies of the dozens of other countries with which they have transactions. They will use as the vehicles for their transactions those national currencies in which they have confidence. They will also accumulate and use working balances in those currencies. The opportunity for traders and bankers to hold and employ vehicle currencies is an essential part of the functioning of the international monetary system.

2. The over-all supply of any national currency—whether it is used only at home, or also as a vehicle currency, or in addition as a reserve currency—will be managed by the central bank or official monetary authority of the country issuing the currency. While this management will be responsive to balance-of-payments discipline, and may be responsive to the implications of criticisms or fears expressed by others, the actual control of a national currency is an attribute of national sovereignty.

3. The criteria for managing the national currencies of most countries, large or small, will be established by the government of each country. These criteria will reflect governmental responsibility both for the domestic economy and for keeping the country in a viable economic relationship with the rest of the world. But from a national point of view it must be expected that monetary control and other elements of economic policy will be limited by the following conditions:

(a) As to prices, there will be little scope for downward flexibility but continuing pressures toward inflation; policy will hope, at best, for reasonable price stability.
(b) As to wages, there will be no practicable scope for reduction but persistent pressure for increases; policy will hope, at best, for a reasonable relationship to productivity gains.
(c) As to employment, while reductions may occur, for seasonal, cyclical or structural reasons, policy will be persistently directed toward achieving the maximum.

The boundaries upon policy, in the present environment, are asymmetrical: strongly biased against deliberate contraction and deflation, and focussed on maintaining balance and curbing excesses.

4. The monetary authorities of most countries will maintain reserves in the form of widely acceptable liquid assets. Because gold has been tested as a store of value through the centuries, while man-made moneys have suffered violent changes, most countries will wish to include some gold in their reserves. They will also wish to be assured that other liquid assets which they hold are readily convertible into gold or will have their equivalent gold value maintained. They look upon gold convertibility as an assurance that the value of any other asset, accepted as a substitute for gold, will be kept reasonably stable. They look upon any acceptable alternative, such as the "maintenance of gold value" commitment to the IMF, as a binding commitment to that stability. They need an anchor of stability to help in checking the inherent pressures for excess that are generated by expanding economies.

5. Most countries will be members of the International Monetary Fund. They will continue to undertake with respect to the IMF an obligation to maintain (and not to impair) the equivalent gold value of the amount of their own currencies that has been paid into the IMF, in terms of the gold-dollar unit originally accepted by the IMF as a standard of value—that is, at the price of $35 per ounce. The IMF will continue to use the cur-

rencies of members, as well as its own gold, in meeting the borrowing needs of other members. Countries whose currencies have been used will, barring offsetting reductions in their other reserves, acquire a corresponding improvement in their reserve positions in the form of an added reserve claim on the IMF. Countries who borrow will expect to repay at maturities determined by the IMF. Repayment will be made in gold, or reserve currencies, or in other currencies acceptable to the IMF.

6. The monetary authorities of each country must, after taking account of credits obtained in the normal course by its business firms and banks, be prepared to meet any sustained net deficits resulting from the combined transactions of that country with the rest of the world. In meeting that need, subject to generally accepted standards of responsible behavior, the monetary authorities will be able to draw upon their own reserves, to draw upon the IMF if the particular country is a member, or to borrow from other monetary authorities as they may agree. If in surplus, a country should be prepared to supply its currency through secure facilities for the financing of other needs or deficits, including use of its currency by the IMF.

These present attributes of the monetary system will come up again for attention throughout the remainder of this book; but their acceptance will be presumed, not debated. These are conditions which have the advantage of familiarity. Traders, bankers, and governments know them and respect them. Their continuance provides a basis for confidence. And without confidence no monetary system could function.

Other Essential Conditions

There are, in addition, other characteristics of the present system that seem to me to be equally essential for the future. One is that the United States must itself maintain the $35 price for an ounce of gold. A second is that the United States must continue to serve as a banker for the world, with the dollar in widespread use both as a vehicle currency and also, at least on the present scale, as a reserve currency. The third is that all leading countries and most other countries should maintain fixed parities for their own currencies. The alternative of fluctuating rates for these countries would cause disruptive chaos, but I will suggest that some of the supposed advantages of fluctuating rates, without the chaos, are already available within the present system.

1. *The necessity of the $35 gold price.*

The dollar, convertible into gold at $35 per ounce, has become the central influence for monetary stability throughout the postwar period. Country after country, having suffered the effects at home and abroad of an erratic but continuing deterioration in the value of its own currency, has made a new start toward stability by defining the par value of its currency in terms of the dollar—a dollar whose convertibility into gold at an unvarying price has remained assured. The fact and the example of that certainty have been intangible but powerful forces in enabling other countries to press for stability in their own monetary affairs. Those forces have in turn been strengthened by the continued impressive performance of the United States economy, and particularly by its ability to combine remarkable expansion with relative price stability.

In turn, the wish of each country to earn dollars and to use them has created a new environment for effective but not rigid accommodation to the necessities of balance-of-payments discipline. These countries found linked with this currency of relatively stable value—a currency that was convertible on demand into gold at a fixed price—an array of credit facilities that enabled their traders, bankers, and governments to supplement their operating balances or their monetary reserves through borrowing in the United States, and to earn interest on balances held in the United States. The dollar became the center of a system that was much more flexible and much more capable of responding to shifting needs than any system based upon gold alone. At the fixed $35 price in terms of gold, the dollar has itself become a tradition. Much of the confidence now gained by many other currencies throughout the world is, in turn, rooted in that tradition.

It has been recognition of the overriding importance of the dollar, both as vehicle currency and as reserve currency for much of the world, that has motivated successive presidents of the United States to renew the assurance that the $35 price would be defended with all necessary means; that the price would, in fact, be immutable. To withdraw that pledge would, in itself, shatter the structure of confidence which has supported the most remarkable expansion of trade among nations in the history of the world—an expansion in which the United States itself has fully shared, and from which its own standard of living has amply gained.

Moreover, if one were to be so cynical or so theoretically inclined as to ignore the obligations which the United States has accepted, there are compelling if more earthy reasons for maintaining the fixed price. One is that the United States, by virtue of its immense size within the trading markets of the world, cannot for the foreseeable future expect to be able to exercise an independent judgment in determining its own exchange rate vis-à-vis the rest of the world. Any attempt to devalue the dollar by writing up the price of gold would assuredly be matched, within hours, by comparable and offsetting action on the part of virtually every other country. The United States would be foreclosed by its size, if it were not already prevented by its committed obligations, from unilateral devaluation. Thus, unable to change its parity against other countries, the United States would find that all that would remain from an increase in the price of gold would be the indicated profit from the markup on whatever was the stock of gold held by the United States at the time.

The act of repudiation and the subsequent spreading of distrust in dollar obligations would surely lead many monetary authorities to convert the dollars still held in their monetary reserves into gold. Indeed, some who have argued for a change in the dollar price of gold have also suggested that the United States should in any event distribute to other official holders an amount of gold (or an equivalent in added dollars) sufficient to compensate for the loss they would have incurred on dollars held at the time of an upward change in the gold price. Whichever the course, the United States would very likely soon be left with no more gold, at the new inflated price, than it had held before the price change occurred. Quite probably, its remaining holdings, even valued at the new higher gold price, would be far less.

To all of this the answer has been given that the United States should instead simply place an embargo on all sales of gold and establish no selling price. In such circumstances, however, the United States would have to buy or sell other currencies in order to maintain the relations which its trade required with other countries and to maintain its parity commitment to the IMF. It would be left then in a position of jockeying over the appropriate exchange rates with other countries. The commitment to supply gold in exchange for dollars would have been abrogated; doubts as to the future attitude of the United States would contribute to speculation; and the anchor of stability for the system would have become unloosened. In these circumstances, some might urge that the United States espouse a system of freely fluctuating rates. That alternative will be critically explored a few pages further on.

Others, quite aware of the hazards that an embargo would create, have suggested instead that the United States, while continuing its fixed selling price at $35, should suspend purchases or make purchases only from time to time on being offered blocks of gold below the $35 price. Such an approach would be in serious conflict with various obligations of IMF members, related to the maintenance of parity within a margin of 1 per cent on either side of the declared par value. While the United States might theoretically switch over to a par value declared in terms of other currencies, rather than gold, there would still be a constraint upon any purchases of gold offered by other members at a price below the gold price implied by their declared parity. To try purposefully to lower the price of gold, the United States would, therefore, at the very least need initial clearance from the IMF.

While much might be said for the salutary effect of a lower gold price upon the schizophrenic tendencies of gold speculators, in practice such an effort on our part alone would probably only result in depriving the United States of a regular inflow of gold that has, over the recent years of travail, been an important offset to the much larger gross volume of outflowing gold that has been purchased from the United States. In 1964, for example, when our net gold sales fell to $125 million (and after allowing for sales to industry and the arts the net outflow was only about $35 million), the United States apparently sold a gross total of close to $1 billion of gold, and published data show purchases of more than $900 million. Most of these purchases came from monetary reserves that were book-valued by their central bank owners at the same $35 selling price as that of the United States. These holdings would simply not have been sold to the United States at any lower price so long as the price at which the United States would in turn sell this gold later on still remained at $35.

More specifically, a "phantom bid" policy would break up the present informal but continuing arrangements through which the United States obtains a substantial part of the net flow of gold reaching the London market from much of the rest of the world. Though we would lose our share, there is no reason to believe that the other countries in the pool would give sufficient credence to the permanence of a lower United States bid to abandon their own buying arrangements, at around the $35 price, if the United States withdrew. The characteristic reluctance of the other larger countries has not been in buying gold, but in selling it. Whether or not they continued activities through the pool in the London market, many of them would undoubtedly be open to offers from sellers anywhere, and willing to buy gold at $35. The spirit of the mercantilists is not dead. The desire for a universally acceptable asset—usable in peace or war, in east or west—is not going to be changed because one minority holder chooses to lower its bid price.

The Common Market countries now hold an aggregate of gold that is equal to the U.S. stock. With the rest of Europe, they far outweigh us. They can "make" the bid price as readily as can the United States, and they have every motive to do so to protect the value of their own holdings. The hard fact is that the United States is no longer in a position to accomplish a lowering of the gold price by unilateral action. The only possibility would be for much of the rest of the world to cooperate in such an attempt, and cooperation in this sphere seems to me most unlikely. The more promising possibility for cooperation, I suspect, lies in progress toward regularizing the gold-holding practices of various central banks. Even here, however, as there will be occasion to mention further in Chapter III, progress will probably occur, if it does, only as part of a complex of other *quid pro quo* relationships.

Moreover, the strength of the assurance provided for the world monetary system by the continuance of the United States selling price would also be undermined if our bid were lowered or withdrawn. Nations would be quick to perceive that gold had become, so far as U.S. reserves were concerned, a continually depleting asset. The technique of the disinterested bid, so often used successfully in poker games or trading markets, would scarcely be credible in the purchasing of gold by a country that, for other compelling reasons, stands ready at all times to sell gold in unlimited quantities at the $35 price. Market acceptance of the certainty of the selling price depends upon market conviction that the seller will have gold to sell.

One final reason for maintaining the existing position of the United States in buying and selling gold at the $35 price is the reinforcement that this gives to the continued role fulfilled by the United States as principal banker for the world. But a review of that complex of considerations leads to the second of the major conditions that I am describing.

2. The continuing role of the United States as world banker.

It has been increasingly common for people in this country to comment, sometimes irritably if not petulantly, that the time has come for the United States to give up its role as world banker. What is it, after all, people ask, that the United States gets from being a reserve currency center, other than severe criticism from abroad and exposure to demands from others for the gold in our own reserves?

It is important to remember the reasons that have thrust the United States into this role, when appraising the costs alongside any possible advantages that might come from attempting to abandon it. The starting point for the dollar as a world currency came from its use in the second of the three major segments of the international monetary system described above—as a trading currency. It was convenient for many, searching for a single currency to serve as a common denominator among transactions in a number of currencies, to use the dollar:

—because the importance of the United States in world trade was itself very large, as seen from most other countries;
—because there were ample and versatile credit facilities available from which supplemental supplies of dollars could be obtained at short term;
—because accumulations held for transactions purposes could be readily invested in liquid form at reasonable rates of return;
—because foreign transactions form so small a part of the vast U.S. markets that foreign holders have little reason to fear that their operations would become conspicuous or subject to interference; and
—because the dollar had an established tradition—honored through various periods of stress—of maintaining open

markets free of the dictation and the intrusions characteristic of exchange control.

The dollar reached its pre-eminent position, of course, during and immediately following World War II when there was in reality no other currency available to play a world role and when so much of our governmental assistance was made available in freely usable dollars. By the time some of the European countries achieved convertibility and large surpluses, the dollar was very deeply entrenched in the usages of trade and payments throughout the world.

It is for many of these same reasons, no doubt, that the dollar will continue to be regarded by most traders and bankers in most countries as a currency they would prefer to use as the vehicle for carrying through their international transactions. That attractiveness will continue to be reinforced as long as the United States, for reasons that would be compelling regardless of its international role, continues to provide the largest and most diversified markets of the world in an environment of steadily rising incomes and of unprecedented price stability. And so long as the American economy remains committed to principles of market freedom, there will be American banks and other financial institutions here eagerly seeking to perform the banking functions identified with the dollar's role as a vehicle currency. From that role, in my view, we cannot in practice withdraw, short of a revolutionary change in our entire economic structure.

Moreover, the provision of services of this kind can reasonably be regarded as a continuing source of income from the balance-of-payments point of view. Not only can the United States as a nation benefit from the income received in performing financial services, but also the inflow of private funds represents a reasonably stable and growing investment item in our own international accounts (although, to be sure, it has customarily been treated for national accounting purposes as a "deficit" item). Over the postwar years, there has been a remarkably regular

increase in outstanding dollar liabilities to foreign private holders, paralleling the advance in aggregate world trade. Thus, unless the United States should take deliberate steps to discourage the use of its own currency in private transactions by the
nationals of other countries, there is likely to be in fact a reasonably permanent growth of foreign investment of this private nature here. The cumulative total of such holdings up through
1964 already amounted to some $11 billion. So long as the habits
and customs of the world continue as they are, there will surely
continue to be a need for increasing amounts of some currency
or other to serve as the vehicle for private transactions. The
dollar will continue as the most likely candidate. It has been
in part as an outgrowth of this role that the dollar reached its
paramount status as a reserve currency.

The present volume of official claims against the dollar
(that is, the extent to which the dollar is being used for reserve purposes by other monetary authorities) now totals more
than $12.5 billion. Should the improbable happen and the
United States decide to indicate (as Switzerland has always done
for its franc) that it is unwilling to have the dollar serve as a
reserve currency, these obligations of $12.5 billion already out-
standing in short-term form to the monetary authorities of
other countries would have to be discharged in some way—and
any way chosen would surely be costly. But beyond that, and
assuming some acceptable substitute were available to meet the
enlarging reserve needs of future years, there would be a great
truncation of the meaningful liquidity now available in the monetary reserves of the world if all these reserve balances were to
be liquidated. If they were to be extinguished, for example,
by a one-for-one disbursement of gold from the United States,
the present total of liquidity lodged in the monetary reserves
of the world would shrink by as much as the $12.5 billion, a
shrinkage of close to one-fifth in the present total of official
liquidity. The immediate burden of the shrinkage would, of
course, fall on the liquidity position of the United States.

These illustrations are, admittedly, extremes that serve principally to illustrate the unwisdom of any abrupt attempt to abandon the dollar's present role, or of taking action that would so disturb the world as to provoke wholesale conversion of dollar reserves into gold. It is also important to weigh, and to weigh heavily, the positive consequences for the prestige and influence of the United States throughout the world that arise from the thousands of individual relationships necessarily created in the day-to-day uses that are made of dollar facilities by traders and bankers and governments in so many other countries. It is the intimacy thus developed that has also helped to encourage a few of the central banks in surplus countries to hold somewhat larger dollar balances than might otherwise have been their intention, as a means of providing a degree of flexibility for the United States as it incurred the kinds of deficits for which financing was required.

There were criticisms, to be sure, as the deficits continued, and understandably so. The users of dollars as reserves did not want to see their reserve assets risk loss of utility through overissue. But without this ready holding of additional dollars, the United States might have been subjected to very severe domestic retrenchment in order to balance its accounts swiftly and avoid default on its obligations. No doubt that would have carried with it correspondingly severe strains for many of our trading partners and for countries that were borrowing heavily in U.S. markets. Nonetheless, there would have been no alternative, given the scale of the deficits the United States was incurring. We did benefit because, as a reserve currency country, we had an array of creditors fully acquainted with our obligations and prepared to absorb a substantial volume of them without negotiation. We have indeed experienced some of the privileges that can go along with the burdens and responsibilities of providing a vehicle currency and a reserve currency for the world.

There may be scope in the future for other reserve currencies, although no other countries have yet been willing to try. And, of course, the world may find other means of fulfilling the needs now met by the dollar. These possibilities raise, however, quite different questions which will be reviewed further in the second and third chapters. The proposition being put here is, quite simply, that the United States should expect to continue providing its dollars for use as a vehicle currency by bankers and traders everywhere; it should expect that the dollar will continue to be used as a reserve currency at least in the magnitudes that have now been reached; and it should be able, through the years, to earn benefits and enjoy privileges that more than offset the strains or burdens associated with these special currency responsibilities.

A case might well be made that many of the supposed burdens or strains are not inherent in the dollar's role in serving others, but are instead the inevitable consequences of the nature of balance-of-payments adjustments in an advanced country—particularly one which has, in many respects, moved out in front of many others and consequently has many awkward problems of phasing and accommodation to resolve in keeping its external accounts reasonably in step with theirs. At any rate, it is complexities of this kind that underline the need of modern economic society for the assured reference points provided by established parities for the rates of exchange among countries, the next condition in the present monetary system that I discuss.

3. The need for fixed rates of exchange.

There is a beguiling appeal in the simple statement of the case advanced for fluctuating exchange rates. For, it is said, rate flexibility is the epitome of free markets. And in any case, it is often added, so long as rates are free to move, they will not move very much; instead they will steady out at the true relationship determined by markets, which are always wiser than bureaucrats. And if at times the rates of exchange on current transactions do not stabilize, there will always be the opportunity of obtaining cover in the forward market so that the individual trader can have the certainty that his business calculations require. Constructive speculation by alert traders will provide adequate facilities for the hedging of risks. Moreover, the fact that exchange rates are free to vary means that, as any one country's external performance slips behind that of most other countries, its exchange rate also begins to slip, giving a clear signal of the need for corrective action without the need to pay out reserves. The world's needs for reserves, so the argument runs, would consequently be much smaller. Concern over the supply of liquidity, either as reserves or as borrowing facilities, would be removed or greatly diminished.

The apparent logic of the scholastic case for fluctuating rates, despite persuasive repetition by able academicians through the years, has never survived the ventilation of experience. Whenever speculation has been encouraged in the free market tradition, more often than not it has been destabilizing so far as exchange rates were concerned. Moreover, public authorities then come under pressure to manipulate the rates, and usually do. This leads to competitive devaluation, and on to trade and exchange restrictions.

But even if they could be left alone, free exchange markets, for all their merits, degenerate into disorderly chaos if they do not have some fixed point of reference. That has, in practice, been provided by the system of fixed exchange rates, and the guidance given to each country, for all other elements of its economic policy, by the need to defend its exchange rate. Rate changes have been made, once a parity was established by any of the major countries, only as discrete moves by individual countries in cases of structural imbalance that could not be corrected through reasonable use of any other instruments of economic policy.

Perhaps a glimpse of what might be involved in reaching a stable base upon which trade could be encouraged is suggested by attempting to visualize the process through which free market rates of exchange would be determined day by day among, say, the United Kingdom, France, and Japan, assuming that rates against all the rest of the world could be ignored and there were no fixed parities. Would any of these three governments, on observing a rise in the exports of its own producers (as their

productivity improved and their prices declined), be prepared to stand by and watch its own exchange rate rise as a
result, ultimately checking its own export growth and thus, as
the theorists promise, limiting the related drain on the reserves
of the others?

If such improbable forbearance were actually practiced,
would the optimum stimulus have been given to sustained
growth in productivity and output throughout all three countries? Or would the impetus of price competition have been lost
or weakened by offsetting changes occurring in the unit of measurement itself? Is this truly a free market for the allocation of
resources when comparative performance cannot be measured
by a uniform standard—when the fact of improvement initiates
offsetting changes in the yardstick by which that improvement
is measured in other countries?

Presumably it is because responsible officials have found
through the years that a general condition of fluctuating rates
would create a sense of rubbery unreality concerning the valid-
ity of all prices that a different choice has been made. Recognizing that fixed exchange rates can only be rough approxi-
mations of the comparative economic positions of various countries, most governments have nonetheless also recognized the
overriding need for a reasonably stable unit of measurement.
Among the leading countries, there was for a time the exceptional case of Canada, but even its experience with a movable
rate only became the exception that proved the rule.

Governments know, too, that their traders cannot function as
well or attempt as much when the normal range of credit risks,
which must be superimposed upon the normal cost comparisons,
is enlarged several times over by uncertainty over the exchange
rates—that is, uncertainty as to the amount of their own currency which they will actually pay or receive when any given
transaction is finally consummated. Only situations with very
high profit margins, capable of covering these extra risks, will
seem attractive. Total world trade will, as a result, be held down.
Whether the risk is carried by the trader himself or shifted by

the trader to the futures market (in the case of those currencies for which an active futures market might exist), the override in cost would necessarily make many transactions prohibitive.

By contrast, a system of fixed rates, hinged as the present system is to a strong center currency and in turn to gold, has its clear reference points. A country that is slipping behind sees the impact, to be sure, in downward pressure on its exchange rate. But its commitment to the IMF to confine fluctuations of the so-called "spot" rate within a margin of 1 per cent on either side of parity means that the country will soon begin using its reserves to "buy in" its own currency. The cue to corrective action will have been given. The length of the period over which the correction can take place will depend in part on the size of the country's reserves or of its access to borrowed reserves—that is, upon its over-all liquidity position. But the country will be in no doubt that it must strengthen its own competitive position by an improved allocation of its own resources. It will have been unambiguously spurred to greater productivity, greater promotion, and greater effort.

Yet there is a grain of truth in the case for fluctuating rates, a grain that need not be lost so long as the primary condition—spot rates close to a fixed parity—is preserved. For there is no specified limit on fluctuations in forward rates; only the arbitrage with spot rates puts a constraint on the range of fluctuations. To be sure, few currencies are in sufficient general use to lead to the continuous maintenance of forward markets in them, but some five to ten such markets have attained significance at different times in recent years. In these markets the same intermediaries, whom our academic friends wishfully expect to make markets under conditions of fully fluctuating rates, would instead buy and sell forward contracts in these currencies. Anyone expecting a change to be made in the official parity of a particular currency, or merely anxious to be fully covered against that risk, could presumably find someone else who was prepared at a price to buy that currency for delivery at a specified future date. As an aside on the easy assumption that forward markets will spring up anywhere, it is interesting to note that, even though this environment for forward trading is much less demanding than that on which traders would have to attempt to quote forward rates on a currency that fluctuates daily over an unspecified range, nonetheless, this presently practicable type of forward trading has not called forth enough ready buyers and sellers to make a forward market for most currencies.

With the development of forward markets for several of the leading currencies, the monetary authorities of those countries have also discovered that a major part of the weight of speculative pressures against a particular currency at times of unsettlement can be shifted on to the forward market for that currency. As a partial alternative to paying out reserves to support its currency in the spot market, the central bank can make forward purchases of its currency—that is, it can promise to use its reserves to purchase its currency at an agreed price at a future date. The result, once the wave of speculation has passed, has often been that the forward seller of the currency finds himself quite satisfied to keep and use it. The forward contract is then unwound; the central bank makes a small profit; the trader has paid a price for protection against exchange risk (in this case the risk that there might be an announced change in the fixed parity); and the central bank has not, with respect to these pressures, had to pay out its reserves.

This is not the use of fluctuating rates that has been visualized by those who view such rates as the full answer for the needs of the international monetary system. They would not find in this the balancing of supply and demand for foreign exchange that they envision as the means to achieving continued balance in the international accounts of each country. But the potentialities to be derived from fluctuations in forward rates, beyond the technical margins of 1 per cent or less that limit the movement of spot rates, can fulfill one of the aims of the proponents of fluctuating rates—namely, helping to conserve the use of monetary reserves. Forward trading can provide certainty through a facility open to anyone who wishes to have absolute protection against the risks, not of widely fluctuating spot rates, but of a single change in the official parity. The central bank can, in turn, by varying the extent of its own intervention in the forward market, allow the cost of this speculative hedge to go as high or as low as it wishes within the range of constraint set by the extent that trading pressures work back upon the spot rate from the forward rate. (That is, if a low quotation for forwards, for example, begins to pull the spot rate to its lower limit, then further lowering of the forward quotation would become self-defeating.)

In effect, a way has been developed for doing what has long been suggested by those who have favored wider margins around the fixed parity for the spot rates as such. A number of practising bankers, including some central bankers, have tried to find a workable compromise between the compelling need they recognize for establishing fixed parities and the desirability which they can see of allowing fluctuations large enough to make disruptive or cumulative speculation costly. The serious risk in any simple widening of the margins surrounding parity for the purpose of current transactions has been that the scope intended for flexible response to temporary influences might also in practice lead to a disguised or unintended change in parity. That is, wider margins might simply mean that some currencies would be allowed to sink close to the lower limit permitted by the lower margin, with such *de facto* devaluation being used as an alternative to the internal corrective measures that would have been required if the spot rate had been kept closer to parity.

The advantage of the present arrangements, as their widened use in recent years has begun to make clear, is that the necessary disciplines of fixed rates can be maintained for the individual countries concerned, while the force of transitional speculation can, at least in significant part, be absorbed through wider swings in the forward markets for the same currency.

Forward operations of this kind would not be practicable for most central banks, however, unless they could feel certain that they could always deliver any foreign currencies needed to meet expiring forward contracts, in case their expectations proved incorrect and the contracts were presented for fulfillment. The central bank must be able to pay for its own currency by delivering the other currency specified in the contract. The necessary backstop, at least initially, for central bank transactions of this kind has been found in the development of standing arrangements to "swap" one's own currency for another by agreement with the central bank issuing the other currency. It was partly for this reason that the United States, beginning in 1961, initiated its ring of bilateral swap agreements with the central banks or monetary authorities of other leading countries. While these swaps have, to be sure, been drawn upon to meet various kinds of short-run swings in reserve needs, their usefulness as a backstop to forward transactions has at times been crucial for the fulfillment of operations that successfully thwarted the cumulative development of speculative pressures against the dollar.

These technical arrangements have been amply described in the various writings of Charles A. Coombs, Vice President of the Federal Reserve Bank of New York, who has been principally responsible for establishing them and has carried out most of the transactions under them in behalf of the United States. Without repeating here any of the record which he has presented so well in the Bank's various publications, it is important to review in a general way the developments that have occurred in recent years in international financial cooperation, of which these swap and forward transactions have been important manifestations.

The Contribution of International Financial Cooperation

Year by year, as the other leading countries have acquired further experience in living with conditions of convertibility for their own currencies, they have become increasingly aware of the intimate interdependence which a convertible system implies for them. There has also been a notable spreading of a sense of shared responsibility for the continued effective functioning of the international monetary system as a whole. With large U.S. deficits beginning by 1960 to appear chronic, a number of countries began to recognize the desirability of enabling the United States to correct those deficits through gradual means that would be lasting in effect, without imposing harsh or sudden retrenchment upon other countries.

One consequence, already noted, was the readiness of some central banks to hold larger dollar balances than their customary practices might have otherwise indicated—mindful that conversions of dollars for gold, if large, could exert an unsettling influence upon many other countries and possibly lead to a disruptive "run" on the dollar. Many were mindful, too, that the United States was fully aware of the need to restore balance, and that anything which precipitated heavy gold conversions was most likely only to persuade the United States that it must, in order to protect its gold reserve as part of its responsibility toward the monetary system, turn to corrective measures for its balance of payments that might put unwelcome strain upon others. Thus, while always assured of convertibility of their dollars into gold on demand at the fixed $35 price, many countries believed that full exercise of such a *privilege* would not be consistent with the degree of *responsibility* which they had come to feel for the continued smooth functioning of the system as a whole. Many, in addition, used some of their accruing dollars to prepay debts owed to the United States. Some used them to acquire U.S. government obligations denominated in their own currencies. Some loaned them to others who were still in urgent need of more dollars for their own reserves.

Another consequence of this growing sense of mutual responsibility was the informal evolution, also mentioned above, of a set of working arrangements among a few of the leading countries for pooling gold to meet any net drain flowing out through the London gold market from monetary reserves, a drain that would otherwise have converged upon the United States alone. In turn, the same countries have shared in any net flow of gold into that market for ultimate absorption into monetary reserves.

On the organizational side there was a reinvigoration of a long-established practice, the monthly gathering of central bank governors and operating officials at the Bank for International Settlements (BIS) in Basle, in which now the United States, and more recently Canada and Japan, regularly participate. A "Working Party 3" was established in 1961 within the new Organization for Economic Cooperation and Development (OECD), bringing together around the same table both Treasury and central bank officials from most of the leading countries at four- to six-week intervals to examine each other's progress toward balance-of-payments equilibrium—to cross-examine, explain, and criticize.

And then, in the event of unusual strains affecting the system as a whole, in order to assure to the IMF an adequate supply of the newly strengthened currencies—alongside the pound and the dollar—the so-called Group of Ten was formed, committed to advance their own currencies in appropriate circumstances up to a total equivalent to $6 billion. From this came additional possibilities for frequent interchange and review, as well as action, by the finance ministers and central bank governors of leading countries meeting together. In turn, these opportunities led to a need for more frequent meetings of their deputies.

In one of the latest phases of this enlarging cooperation the Group of Ten initiated a wide-reaching study in the autumn of 1963 into the functioning and future needs of the international monetary system. This accompanied a corresponding analysis in the 1964 *Annual Report* of the IMF. Although the work of the Group of Ten is still continuing in 1965, the study did yield an initial report after its first stage in the summer of 1964.

The resulting Ministerial Statement and Annex Prepared by Deputies are reproduced in the Appendix beginning on page 131. They demonstrate, more clearly than could any brief summary here, the extent to which, and the directions in which, these countries have begun to work together to strengthen the international monetary system. They also provide implicit evidence of the kinds of differences that have arisen among these countries and of the direct manner in which these differences are being forthrightly debated within official circles. Conflicts, some of them sharp, have occurred in all of the forums of cooperation. Had conflicts not occurred in dealing with issues that penetrate into the differing national objectives of the various sovereign countries, there could be little hope for progress.

International cooperation, when meaningful, is no tea party, as Elihu Root knew so well. But it does require frank confrontation, continuous communication, and a readiness for negotiation when the time is right. In these respects, the new international financial cooperation, of which the work of the Group of Ten is one prominent evidence, has advanced the world far beyond the stage that Elihu Root, or the statesmen of the entire interwar period, walked upon.

As the Appendix indicates, one fundamental area of disagreement and concern was that relating to the elements of the adjustment process, as nations in varying stages of development attempt to maintain viable balance-of-payments positions. The Group of Ten recognized their own primary responsibility for much more systematic analysis of the essentials of the adjustment process among industrialized countries under conditions of convertibility. That task was assigned to the OECD's Working Party 3, which had by 1964 acquired several years of experience in keeping close watch on problems of current imbalance, and which at this writing is testing out the possibilities for more systematic definition of the measures and the responsibilities that deficit and surplus countries should be expected to undertake over the years ahead.

Paralleling this search for more regularized criteria, in order to speed adjustment and in turn reduce somewhat the potential magnitudes of future liquidity needs, the first report of the Group of Ten also recommended the establishment of a closer watch—it was called "multilateral surveillance"—over the ways in which deficits are financed and surpluses are used. This task was assigned by the ministers and governors directly to themselves, with responsibility for detailed review expected to be carried not only by the IMF itself but also by the Basle Group, Working Party 3, and the deputies of the Group of Ten. To assure coordination, a virtually full overlap of country memberships was provided for all these groups, and members of the staffs of the BIS, the IMF, and the OECD were given permanent places in all of them as well. The BIS was asked to serve as confidential clearing house for the systematic assembling of all the necessary data on the current financing of deficits and the uses of surpluses by each of the participating countries.

Here, then, for those who are concerned over the possibility of abuse and excess, or of abstinence and contraction, in the uses of liquidity is one important route toward the multilateralizing of meaningful responsibility. And from the continuing debates and disagreements that should characterize effective "multilateral surveillance" will also come experience to condition the work of another group, working directly under the Deputies of the Group of Ten, to analyze the pros and cons of the many proposals that have been made for reform of the international monetary system.[1]

In all of these various undertakings, and in work that continues daily in the IMF, the OECD, the BIS, and in other groups, there are undoubtedly very important seeds for that further evolution of the system which will be the subject of the next two chapters—an evolution toward broader sharing among nations of the responsible action needed for peace, progress, and stability on the monetary front, a responsibility that no one nation can or should, in monetary or in political affairs, be expected to manage alone.

[1] This committee, under the Chairmanship of Rinaldo Ossola of the Bank of Italy, reportedly presented its findings to the Deputies at the end of May 1965.

II

THE OBJECTIVES OF
MONETARY REFORM

The Contradictory Motives for Reform

INTEREST in international monetary reform began to mount following the return of convertibility among most of the industrialized countries at the end of 1958. That was no accidental coincidence. Throughout all the preceding years since World War II, attention had necessarily been focussed first on basic reconstruction and then later on achieving the conditions that would permit these countries to undertake the obligations of "current account" convertibility for their own currencies. For some fourteen years the nations accounting for the bulk of the world's trade and payments had only been moving toward the initiation of the system that had been envisioned at Bretton Woods in 1944. Not until that objective had been achieved by a considerable number was it possible in 1959 to begin testing the capabilities of a convertible system against the actual requirements of a rapidly expanding, and almost bewilderingly diversified, world economy.

Over much of the pre-convertibility period, the United States had provided the extra margin of resources which others needed to sustain their own efforts to reach the threshold of convertibility. Once convertibility had been established by most of the industrialized countries, the United States continued to provide both real resources and additional liquidity to support, and in a sense to lubricate, their accommodation to the newly established mechanism. While U.S. dollars provided the largest part of the actual increase in primary reserves, dependence upon the credit facilities of the IMF also grew increasingly. But differences in the pace of advance among the IMF's member countries, and the frictions encountered as each attempted to mesh its own continually changing economic gears with those of the changing economies surrounding it, created strains for some, frustrations for others, and a series of unsettling financial disturbances, bordering on crisis, for important segments of the international financial system.

By 1961 the United States found that the facilities it had created for strengthening the world economy, and the diversified financial markets which had equipped it to serve as the principal reserve currency, were being utilized on a scale so large that the United States itself seemed unable to achieve balance in its own external accounts. What had happened, paradoxically, was that the capabilities which had nourished the growth of much of the rest of the world had begun, in a relative sense, to sap the foreign economic strength of the United States. Successive deficits occurred in every year following the return of convertibility.

The continuation of these deficits, substantial losses of gold by the one country that was maintaining the gold anchor needed for a stable monetary system, and the development of inflationary conditions throughout much of Europe, all combined to create an atmosphere of uneasiness in which appeals for reform flourished. One of the first requirements in the circumstances, of course, was that the United States bring its own accounts back to balance. This, in its own interest and in the interest of world stability, it must do in an orderly manner, without disruptive repercussions on the trade, the financial markets, or the balance-of-payments positions of others. While accomplishing the corrective adjustment, it should also finance its remaining transitional deficits in ways that would, as fully as possible, contribute to the further constructive evolution of the new convertible system.

The record of that effort of the United States from 1961 through 1964, and the analysis upon which the governmental aspects of that effort rested, have been described often in various official papers. Some of the financial innovations of the period have already been mentioned in the preceding chapter; others will be touched upon shortly. But I shall reserve for another volume any attempt I might make toward a more extensive review of the dollar in relation to world liquidity over those four years. What matters for the analysis of reform proposals here is simply a straightforward recognition from the start that dollar viability must be re-established. No reform can take the place of correction in the balance of payments of this country. Once that is clear, there is a reasonable basis for going ahead to examine some of the various motives which have given rise to suggestions for reform.

There should be no surprise that the chorus of calls for monetary reform over the past few years has not resulted in ready agreement on action. For the calls have come from such different positions that any attempt to begin specific discussion, much less international negotiation, has quickly revealed a clash of objectives among those urging reform. And most of the reformers themselves, as has so often happened in the history of reform efforts, have been intensely present-minded, finding their cause for change in immediate circumstances which they consider to be inherent consequences of "the system."

There are many ways in which their different approaches may be catalogued. Without trying to relate any of them to specific plans, I think it is helpful in searching out the possible scope for constructive change to look briefly at six different, and somewhat conflicting, sets of motives for urging serious reform of the present monetary arrangements.

1. *End the overexpansion of reserve currencies.*

Some of the critics, and these have been mainly from surplus countries recently undergoing inflationary pressure, have felt that a reserve currency system by its nature necessarily generates too much liquidity. The United States, they believe, cannot resist taking undue advantage of its position as the principal source of created reserves. Because it has run large deficits every year since the return of convertibility, it can be expected, as a rule, to run larger deficits for longer periods than other countries could contemplate. The deficits of a reserve currency country draw more real resources from the creditor countries, in goods received or investments acquired, than it returns to them. The unrequited balance in favor of the reserve currency country may, they argue, help to offset any inflationary tendencies within that country—as it receives good assets in exchange for the currency it issues—but the creditor countries are left with unduly large holdings of reserve currencies, a potentially inflationary growth in the domestic credit base, and an inflationary gap between their volume of domestic spending and the volume of domestic resources remaining available for purchase.

The objective, as many of these critics see the need, should be to halt the use of reserve currencies. Some would do that by establishing a "pure" gold standard; others, by establishing new facilities for the controlled creation of reserve assets by some multinational group. But the basic aim of many, and it deserves frank consideration, is to find an effective way to end, or greatly modify, the unique role of the United States in the creation of international liquidity. For a few critics this aim may be intertwined with a political antipathy, but for most it is instead the prudent concern that any businessman or banker feels when heavily dependent upon one client—his reliable instinct is to seek a diversification of risks.

2. Enlarge the capacity for liquidity creation.

At the other extreme there are those, found mainly among the deficit countries or the less developed countries, who believe that liquidity is far too small to permit adequate expansion of their own economies and of the flows of world trade and capital. Gold production is certainly too small; but these critics add that reserve currencies must necessarily, because they are the obligations of single countries, be administered too cautiously to allow ample growth. Recognizing that part of the problem they see may be one of the distribution of reserves and of borrowing facilities, they nonetheless insist that an over-all shortage is the principal deficiency of the system. At a time of great potentials, they see expansion stifled by the monetary system. Because countries naturally want to avoid default on their obligations, and because they do not have enough liquidity to meet the deficits incurred when expanding domestic incomes enlarge import demands, deficit countries have to achieve balance in their foreign accounts by retrenchment. The costs are the intermittent slackening of the national economy and a volatility in foreign trade that interferes with world-wide growth.

The answer, seen from this side of the reform platform, should be larger continuing increases in liquidity—possibly through a steep rise in the price of gold, or the introduction of a multinational reserve currency, or the large-scale expansion of credit extended to deficit countries through the IMF or in some other way, or some combination among these possibilites. A few of these advocates hurt their cause, however, by posing the needs on such a grandiose scale as to create fear of a breakdown of values and payments arrangements in an epidemic of inflationary excess.

3. *Reduce the strain on reserve currencies.*

Another kind of call for more liquidity or for new liquidity arrangements has come mainly from within the reserve currency countries themselves, particularly the United Kingdom but also the United States. Both as vehicle and as reserve currencies, the argument runs, the pound and the dollar are subject to unusual strains and drains causing frequent and severe interference with American or British domestic objectives for employment, income, and living standards. Any widespread uncertainty concerning political or economic conditions around the world, as well as any doubt concerning the balance-of-payments positions of the reserve currency countries themselves, can lead to sudden changes in the world-wide readiness to hold their currencies—a kind and degree of exposure which other countries, whose currencies are not outstanding in large amounts outside their own borders, would never undergo.

Moreover, as reserve needs grow over time the exposure of the dollar, at least, would by arithmetic necessity become greater. As the ratio of dollars to gold increased, even if the total were generally considered appropriate, there would be a steady attrition of the U.S. gold holdings. Each wave of uncertainty would cause some precautionary withdrawals; and with gold relatively scarce, countries would be less and less likely to return gold to the United States after acquiring it. And as other countries grow, each may wish or expect to have some increase in the absolute amount of its gold holdings, and the relative holdings of the United States would decline for that reason as well.

The solution, some critics would say, is to drop the reserve currency responsibility altogether, persuading the world to adopt some new kind of internationalized reserve unit for general use. Others, not going that far, would argue that additional ways should be found for other countries to extend more support to the reserve currencies. Some responsible central bankers have indeed suggested, for example, that countries adopt uniform practices for combining within their reserves fixed proportions of gold and reserve currencies, and possibly other assets. There have also been suggestions that some of the substantial surplus countries grant large, long-term credits to the reserve currency countries as a means of underwriting a part of the common facility which the reserve currencies provide—in effect funding or "consolidating" part of the pound and dollar liabilities, possibly at intervals of fifteen or twenty years. While either or both of these burden-sharing approaches would help to reduce pressures on the reserve currencies and possibly accomplish some diversification of risks, there would also presumably be some other "performance bond" expected from the reserve currency countries. For that, some have suggested exchange or gold guaranties. While selective versions of either have been successfully used, through the IMF or in swap arrangements, for example, other versions are quite capable of undermining rather than strengthening confidence in the acceptability and reliability of a reserve currency. It will be necessary in pursuing these suggestions, as in so many other aspects of monetary arrangements, to distinguish between attractive objectives urged in good faith and the implied but unintentional consequences of a harmful nature. I shall try to do that later in this book.

4. Transfer excess idle reserves to active uses.

Quite a different concern, not heard as often as the others, relates to the absorption of liquidity by countries in chronic surplus. While the correction of sustained surpluses is more properly regarded as part of the adjustment process, the uses of surpluses do affect the scale of over-all liquidity needs. There should be some method, it is argued, for putting back into general use the redundant holdings of reserves by those surplus countries which do not otherwise put their reserves to work by permitting increases in their own imports, or enabling outsiders to borrow in their markets, or expanding their own investment abroad, or undertaking grants in aid of the less developed countries. In such cases there should be a ready facility, and a recognized obligation, for the country in chronic surplus to transfer its excess holdings of gold and dollars (or sterling) to the IMF or some other central pool of liquid resources, presumably to receive in return a gold guaranty of their value. Another approach, less subject to the risk just mentioned of discrediting the reserve currencies, would be for a non-reserve-currency country to lend its own currency or deposit it in the IMF, in the expectation that the ultimate recipient would in turn present that currency to the issuing central bank for exchange into, say, usable sterling or dollars already held in that central bank's reserves.

To be sure, one may rightly ask when these suggestions are made, how far any system can go, or should go, in providing such an alternative secure lodgment for the accumulations of countries in surplus. And if there were to be deposits withdrawable at will, one might ask whether these could be effectively used by, say, the IMF. By analogy, capital accumulation in the private sector would be sterile indeed if those able to accumulate did not also recognize that they have a responsibility—to themselves, and for the continuation of a prospering world round about them—to hold some long-term investments, i.e., to diversify their holdings, not merely among different riskless instruments of liquidity, but also among other kinds and maturities of assets which, while mobilizable in case of real need, can be considered intramarginal from the standpoint of pure liquidity. In the handling of official reserves such diversification would be comparable, for example, to the three-part classification into primary, secondary and tertiary reserves that has been in use for some time in Italy, where so much of the creative innovation in monetary management has occurred over the past twenty years.

5. *Install automatic arrangements to supply liquidity.*

Another approach to reform would question any arrangements that make the supply of liquidity depend upon variable human action and judgment, year by year. According to this argument, the world needs instead an assured and steady growth in its money supply. It must agree initially on the technical arrangements and on the growth rate; but then, as with a municipal water-works, once installed, the regular provision of a steady flow of liquidity can be assured by an engineer who keeps the machinery in repair. This view is an international counterpart of the "quantity of money" school in domestic economic analysis. The proposal would be for the establishment of an international currency-creating unit, committed from the beginning to produce a fixed percentage increase of reserves each year, with all countries committed to hold these reserve units and to accept them in official settlements with each other—presumably to the exclusion of other reserves.

The desire is quite understandable to rely upon simple automaticity as a means of avoiding both the mistakes and the excesses of money management. Yet, even side-stepping the practical details of setting up an automatic mechanism that would just "go on working" once put in place, there would be in such an approach the possibility that initial errors of judgment at the beginning stage could set off a juggernaut. To be sure, the changes or additions to the system that come from reform should, if at all possible, be kept simple; but they must continually be subject to further change as the world environment changes. That is why, of course, no individual country has ever domestically been able to commit itself to continuous automatic increases in its own money supply. Even the rare instances of attempts by central banks to set annual targets for change in the money supply have been subject to continuous correction as significant developments occurred. That is why the institutions of Bretton Woods were designed for adaptation, and to be built upon. That is why the possibilities for reform can be, and need to be, discussed today; the world has allowed itself room for change. Perhaps the prerequisite for any reform should be that it does not depend upon irrevocable and irreversible commitments that virtually exclude all other possibilities for reform later on.

6. *Substitute consciously guided reserve creation for present unguided arrangements.*

The final "school of thought" in this list is not attracted by any purely automatic facility; it wants a managed supply of international liquidity, but it considers the present management incomplete and inadequate. It can embrace proposals of various kinds—some that would displace reserve currencies, others that would merely supplement them. Its essential requirement is for an internationalized decision-making process through which changes can be made at the margin, to determine in any given conditions how much more should be added, or how much taken away, from the current supply of monetary reserves. In some versions, this over-all discretion is also extended to include control over the provision of those credit facilities through which existing reserves, once created, may be exchanged among countries to increase the intensity of their use.

In viewing the three sectors of the international monetary system, this school of criticism sees a reasonably satisfactory degree of reliance upon money management at the national level. With respect to the "vehicle currency" requirements, most of these critics are generally content that the competing private credit facilities are capable of assuring an adequate availability of financing for international trade and an adequate supply of currencies, mainly dollars, for the transactions balances of traders and bankers abroad. They see this part of the system as largely self-administering, with any risk of over-extension of credit taken care of by the internal monetary controls of the countries that finance international trade. But they are concerned about the supply of dollars for monetary reserves (alongside gold and sterling). These sources of supply, they feel, are subject to arbitrary and partly accidental influences unrelated to monetary needs for reserves and cannot be relied upon to provide an adequate volume of fully acceptable assets in the future. They may provide too little, or too much—the world cannot be sure which.

Whether concerned because there have been too many reserve dollars in the past, or because the United States may either provide not enough or too much in the future, or for all such reasons, these critics believe that determination of the supply of reserve assets will always be at issue between countries which are currently in surplus and those in deficit. Moreover, the management of that supply, or of marginal changes in it, will in the future be too controversial and too important to be lodged in any one country.

The prudent banker or businessman, whose confidence any system must retain, would probably agree on the need for diversification of responsibility. But it is important to realize that the United States is not, even now, a free agent; that checks and balances are at work, giving every country a voice and an opportunity to bring pressure on the United States through the way in which that country handles any dollars accruing in its own official reserves. To be sure, during the period of convertibility since 1958, some countries have been very sensitive to the system-wide implications of their actions and have exercised their "voting" influence cautiously, relying on persuasion rather than on leverage to induce the United States to cut down the outflow of dollars through its deficits. Other countries have alternated, sometimes acting to cushion pressures and sometimes acting or speaking out aggressively to help force restrictive action. Still others have simply acted without regard to the impact of their actions on the dollar or its gold reserves. In accordance with the assumptions of earlier years that each could consider itself too small a part of the total to have any influence individually upon the performance of the system as a whole, they have looked only to their own situation. They have not been at all self-conscious over exercising any privilege open to them.

The position of the critics is that this variation in the exercise of national influence can also be damaging, leading to undue domination by the more extreme or the less restrained countries, and that a more orderly representation of all—large and small, industrial and developing—should be assured in the procedures for determining the amount of liquidity creation. That, of course, has been a major motive for regularizing the many-sided arrangements for multilateral surveillance which the United States has welcomed—not the least of these being the annual "Article VIII" review of the United States conducted by the IMF since 1962. But the critics seem to want more.

The Scope for Adaptation, Short of Reform

Even the cursory summary given above is enough to demonstrate that the only view held in common among the various proponents of reform is that something must be changed. Could they be set to work, they would surely get in each other's way—each contradicting or offsetting much of the force of another. Yet the combined effect of an appraisal of all these complaints is not a simple cancelling of terms on both sides of an equation, leaving nothing to change. On one side, there does emerge from a sorting out of these criticisms a series of misunderstandings concerning both the way in which the present system already functions and the relatively simple changes which could greatly strengthen this system without turning to extensive reform. Yet on the other side, a number of criticisms and objectives still remain unfulfilled and can probably be satisfied only by genuine reform, provided the reform would not at the same time impair the fundamentals of the system that were described in the first chapter. The balance of this chapter will attempt a further sorting out, focussing mainly on the scope for adaptation short of reform, but then going on to outline the areas that seem still to remain open—areas within which there would seem to be room for further reform without toppling any of the essential pillars of the present arrangements.

1. *The continuing use of vehicle currencies.*

Few of the cases for reform give any attention to the implications of the fact that some currencies—and given the nature of the need it will only be a very few—will always be needed as vehicles for use in ordinary international transactions. This is the need that may in fact grow in some rough correspondence with the growth in world trade. As I suggested earlier, this crucial segment of the international monetary system, essential for the promotion and the servicing of trade, will probably require dollars, and most likely sterling, for as far ahead as planning can be meaningful.

The choice of dollars is, at least in part, a by-product of the fact that the United States is the world's largest trading country. The relationship between foreign-held, non-official dollar balances and the total volume of world trade (exports plus imports, but excluding the Communist bloc) has remained between 3 and 3½ per cent through every year since the return of convertibility. And as foreign holdings of transactions balances in dollars keep on growing there will also, as a corollary, be some growth in the dollar needs of central banks, for monetary authorities have routine transactions of their own to conduct, and transactions to execute in the foreign-exchange markets with private traders. They will undoubtedly continue to require some dollar balances in their reserves, whatever the future may bring in terms of alternative holdings.

Unless and until one or two more of the national currencies grow into comparable widespread use and develop internal financial markets equal to the tasks of servicing a world-wide currency, it would seem that the world must have dollars—for its transactions and to some extent for its reserves—if its trade is to flourish. That means that any changes or reforms in the system as a whole should be compatible with the continued provision of dollars for trading needs. This end will be furthered, and misunderstanding abroad avoided in the future, if there is at least one official measure of the United States balance-of-payments deficit that does not include the steadily growing volume of private holdings of liquid dollars, as the Bernstein committee has recently recommended.[1]

To be sure, the line between private and official holdings of dollars is never sharp, and changes in the size of foreign-held private dollar balances can never be ignored in appraising the balance-of-payments performance of the United States. But the arteries of trade could harden if, to take a prime example, American banking credits that are extended to carry foreign trade must always be stigmatized in the official records as deficits as soon as the dollars pass into the account of the foreigner who has need for them. Yet the total of such dollars, though represented by a continuing shift among the underlying credits, has increased and presumably will go on increasing every year. Neither the statistical procedures of our own government nor any substantive reform of the monetary system itself should be so designed as to imply a need to cut off the dollars that the world will continue to need for transactions purposes.

[1] *The Balance of Payments Statistics of the United States,* Report of the Review Committee for Balance of Payments Statistics to the Bureau of the Budget (Washington: GPO, April 1965), pp. 2-3.

2. *Is monetary reform needed to curb excessive United States deficits?*

If there is then any basis for the first of the six complaints—i.e., the charge that the United States has evaded balance-of-payments discipline and spread inflation in Europe by financing its large deficits with created dollars that surplus countries reluctantly accepted—that basis must relate to the reserve currency part of the story. Even here, observation from a distance may distort the picture. For the increase in U.S. liabilities to foreign official accounts, though always apparently an object of envy when viewed from abroad, has been accompanied by an intensification of corrective effort within this country.

To the U.S. authorities, these liabilities did not appear as a mere financing of a current deficit, but as the added margin of debt, superimposed on an already large total, that might unsettle a part of these already large existing obligations and precipitate a cumulative loss of gold—damaging both for continued confidence in the monetary system and for our own long-range need to maintain liquid reserves. These increasing dollar liabilities were in themselves actually a goad to more penetrating and determined action to shrink the deficit progressively to zero—a process which has continued with intensifying effort, and reasonably satisfactory results, although the bursting of new leakages along the way sometimes made the over-all totals seem to respond quite slowly. And, of course, those surplus countries which were nervous over their own accruals had at any time the options of reducing import restrictions, or of taking offsetting financial measures at home, or using their surpluses to invest more abroad, or even making foreign grants.

The case that rests on United States laxity is not by any means a persuasive one. Indeed, despite its supposed reserve currency advantage, the United States lost (net) about $6 billion of gold over the first six years of convertibility, while its supposed "free ride" (its liabilities to official foreign holders) went up considerably less, about $4 billion. And so far as can be determined, official liabilities to Western Europe as a whole (net of various special arrangements, to be sure) actually dropped significantly in 1963 and 1964. Nonetheless, it must be granted that a risk of laxity exists. And more broadly, the world may understandably feel uneasy for the future when the crucial marginal additions to the supply of monetary reserves depend upon the policies and the balance-of-payments position of one country, or upon the pressures that may be applied against that country by as few as one or two others.

Short of reform or until it comes, however, this is by no means a hopeless situation. There is not, at least not because the international monetary system is presently hinged so closely to the dollar, any inevitable crisis just ahead that calls for immediate action—important as it is to push forward now to work out the blueprints of useful future change. For the immediate future it is necessary, and quite possible, to hold the U.S. balance-of-payments position very close to zero, or perhaps in surplus, by whatever method this measurement is made. Any alarmist pressure for reform from the surplus countries may be expected to quiet down to the slower tempo of responsible concern when the continuing demands for dollars to be used in ordinary private transactions are no longer being satisfied from the United States but instead begin to draw away those redundant central bank reserves in Europe that have so recently seemed disturbing. And over recent months such a drain has apparently begun. That must continue.

Once the sense of dollar scarcity is restored, there is still no reason to fear an early reversion to either too much reserve creation or too little. For one reason, under the overlapping arrangements for multilateral surveillance described at the close of the preceding chapter, the financial officials of the leading industrial countries (joined by the staffs of the IMF, the OECD, and the BIS) have already mounted watch on a continuing basis over the surpluses or deficits of each other, and the way in which each is financed. No sovereignty has been sacrificed; but because of the frequent and full exchange of confidential data on balance-of-payments developments, and on the financing methods that each country is using, there is no longer any serious likelihood that the United States could, unknowingly or unconcernedly, impose the financing of any substantial deficits of its own upon other countries without their knowledge and against their will. Whenever the group as a whole or several among the group see serious cause for concern, the channels are established and open for prompt and orderly official communication based on data now assembled from both the deficit and the surplus sides.

The people of the United States will surely never forget the lessons of a completely new experience which they needed several years to learn: that in the new circumstances of convertibility, and surrounded by many other strongly advancing countries, the United States must give a leading priority to its balance-of-payments position in determining its over-all economic policy. It has to maintain a viable relationship with the rest of the world in real terms. External financing, whether through the "forced saving" imposed on others by generating an excess of dollars or through explicit borrowing, cannot be a substitute for, nor an alternative to, real correction of a balance-of-payments deficit. Financing, suitably adapted to the positions of other countries and drawing upon their real resources at a pace which they can readily accommodate, can provide the time for orderly correction; it cannot remove the need for correction. Where balance-of-payments adjustment is concerned, there is no Santa Claus—no escape in the guise of liquidity. These facts are widely known now and widely understood in the United States. It is most improbable that large deficits could be allowed to develop to disruptive proportions in the future, whether or not the United States were to continue as a principal supplier of monetary reserves for the world.

3. *Is monetary reform needed to assure adequate liquidity?*

With the initial effects of a tightened U.S. balance-of-payments program already being felt as this is written, current apprehension seems to center more upon the risk of inadequate liquidity than upon that of oversupply. Before appraising that risk of inadequacy, however, I want to note here, with a promise to return to the matter subsequently, the absolute necessity of distinguishing carefully between the reserves and the credit facilities which constitute liquidity, on the one hand, and the flows of aid or investment funds which so many countries urgently need, on the other. There is an irrefutable case for development aid, and there are ways of extending some aid as a counterpart of the creation of reserves. But a justifiable need for additional aid does not of itself justify the creation of additional reserves.

Appraisal of the adequacy of reserves, or of the credit facilities through which reserves can be loaned or borrowed, rests upon a judgment of monetary requirements: that is, (a) the total quantity of the medium of exchange that central banks need, at prevailing prices, to make all the reserve transfers or purchases of their own currency in the exchange markets that are necessary as a consequence of the payments arising out of the flows of trade, or capital, or aid that the world is undertaking; and (b) the cumulative total of the balances that central banks are able and willing to hold to meet various swings in these requirements and to meet contingency requirements. However carefully managed the supply of liquidity may be toward the fulfillment of these monetary needs, such management must not be expected to include a "forced levy" to provide additional development aid by superimposing additional cash balances upon the central banks of the creditor countries.

If development aid, with all its merits, can then be set aside for the present, the two-part question is whether a constricting shortage of liquidity is about to set in, and whether the imminence of that shortage requires early reform of the international monetary system. My own answer is, no, on both counts, but that does not mean that I see no case for reform to assure an adequacy of reserves in the future.

The first point to be made in present circumstances is that liquidity does consist of two very large components; there are the reserves, and there are the credit facilities. Over the decade from the end of 1953 to the end of 1963, for example, as shown in the table accompanying the interim report of the Deputies of the Group of Ten reproduced in the Appendix, there was a measurable growth in over-all liquidity of some $27 billion, of which about $6 billion came from an increase in monetary gold, $8 billion from the increase in official holdings of foreign exchange, mainly dollars, and $13 billion, or roughly half of the total, from the increase in activated credits and in assured and negotiable credit facilities, including quotas at the IMF. Moreover, it could well be argued, and I acknowledge that in my former role at the Treasury Department I have so argued, that the world is nearing the close of a period of rapid increases in reserves, that some time may be needed fully to absorb these reserves, and that the current phase is more appropriately one for expansion in the provision of credit facilities (such as the 1965 increase in IMF quotas) and in the use of such facilities (such as the large drawings by the United Kingdom in November 1964 and May 1965).

But there are other important offsets to any balancing in U.S. accounts that would shut off the flow of dollars into the world. One, which has already been noted, is that some of the presently large central bank holdings of dollars can and should be paid out in order to supply the continuing growth in the transactions requirements for dollars by the traders and banks of the world. That would serve at the same time to resist any contractionary tendencies abroad set off by the shrinkage of dollars flowing from this country. In addition, should any serious squeeze become apparent in private trade, that could be met by permitting an increase of private dollar credits from the United

States, provided that there was a widespread recognition and expression of such a need outside the United States and that no increase in the U.S. deficit to official accounts were to result (i.e., no "Bernstein deficit"). So far as the vehicle currency requirements are concerned, consequently, there need be no significant problem.

With respect to reserve needs, any marked shortage is presumably many months, probably years, away. If it should begin, however, before any agreement had been reached on other supplementary forms of reserves, and if credit facilities were not considered adequate, the simplest first step would be for the IMF to borrow on its own initiative from members with large reserves and, in turn, to pay out these currencies to drawing countries which would presumably convert them into dollars for actual use.

Should that step fail, the IMF could revert to a full use of dollars in meeting new drawings. The world's supply of dollars would increase in response to clearly defined needs that had been carefully reviewed in the highest forum of international finance. And the United States would be restoring its own position in the IMF. Every dollar drawn would reduce the existing United States debt to the IMF by a corresponding amount and release an equal amount of its gold tranche for virtually automatic use by the United States in the future. When that debt was retired, further drawings of dollars would begin building U.S. reserves in the form of "super gold tranche" claims upon the IMF.

Should the use of dollars by the IMF be less than enough, or proceed too slowly, there would still be other alternatives. The United States could, if requested, redeem for dollars some of its outstanding bonds denominated in the currencies of the creditor countries to which they were issued. Or further, the United States could begin to add to its own supply of convertible foreign currencies, under arrangements to be agreed upon with the issuing central banks, and in turn supply these central banks with dollars for their own needs. Any such transactions should, of course, be fully disclosed to the other leading currency countries which participate in the multilateral surveillance of the financing arrangements of each other, and should presumably be carried out only after discerning general agreement that a further enlargement of over-all liquidity in this way was appropriate and was not likely to be promptly offset by corresponding increases in purchases of gold from the United States.

There would also be the possibility, in response to general indications of such wishes abroad, that the United States could take steps to reduce any surplus being accumulated on an "official settlements" (Bernstein) basis, even at the risk of incurring a modest deficit. Gradual relaxation of the various restrictive measures that had helped achieve balance and surplus would, in those circumstances, presumably prove constructive in various ways. Depending on priorities then apparent and restraints then in effect, voluntary credit restrictions could be relaxed or lifted; the interest equalization tax could be modified or terminated; uneconomic and unwelcome limitations on our overseas military establishment could be relaxed; the tying of aid could be loosened or eliminated; the limits on duty-free imports could be raised. The list is long; the prospect of action on some or all is indeed appealing.

Through these various approaches, and without any unilateral indulgence in laxity, there should be ample scope for handling any clear need for additional reserves over the years immediately ahead—once the experience of "dollar shortage" has removed the scarlet letter that some have overprinted on the dollar in the past few years.

4. Can monetary reform reduce strains on the reserve currencies?

The unique strains on reserve currencies arise at least partly because of the large outstanding volume of those currencies in other hands, which then amplify the impact of any upsetting development—whether that be a military incident affecting prospects for peace in the world, for example, or a banking failure somewhere, or a deterioration in the balance-of-payments position of the reserve country itself. Thus it is inherent in the purposes for which reserve currencies are widely held by other countries that there will be more frequent and more intensive pressures upon those currencies in the foreign-exchange markets than upon others, and a greater likelihood that cumulative forces of speculation will be set off against currencies widely held outside their own country.

Since the pound and more particularly the dollar will surely be used as vehicle currencies and to some extent as reserves, it is critically important, whatever else may happen to the monetary system in the future, to develop methods for minimizing the strains upon these currencies. And even if, in the longer reaches of evolutionary change, the French franc or the German mark or a common currency for the Common Market, for example, were to share the position now occupied by the pound or the dollar, the basic need to provide some support for the currencies that are widely used would remain. That support should come through the joint effort of those other leading currencies which, while benefitting directly and indirectly from the services performed, are not in a position to furnish comparable services themselves.

No doubt, any change that could be introduced in the creation of reserve assets in the future would moderate the piling up of still further strains on the currencies now used as reserves, but that kind of assistance is not likely to be enough. That is one of the reasons why it was essential beginning in 1961 for the United States to establish a ring of bilateral swap arrangements with all the other leading currencies, and that is why this ring should be regarded as a permanent addition to the new convertible monetary system, and why increases should occur from time to time in the agreed swap lines with other strong currencies. The total facilities already negotiated have now reached $2.65 billion, or close to $2 billion if the $750 million swap agreement with the other reserve currency, the pound sterling, is excluded. It is most probable, moreover, that in case of unexpected developments the existing facilities could be swiftly enlarged through telephone agreement between central banks that have already acquired extensive experience in the appropriate uses of these arrangements.

Apart from the backstopping of forward contracts mentioned above, which these swap lines have helped to assure (generally without being drawn upon, in practice), the lines also give the United States assurance that it can in the course of a telephone call, in quick-breaking circumstances, draw the equivalent of many hundreds of millions of dollars in other currencies for use in resisting speculative pressures against the dollar. That is what was done, for example, when the world was stunned on the Friday afternoon of November 23, 1963, by the assassination of President Kennedy. A shocked world, in which prudent holders of foreign exchange had to consider the prospect of a deteriorating position in the United States, was reassured insofar as the standing of the dollar in world markets was concerned by the instantaneous posting of offers by the Federal Reserve Bank of New York—offers to sell any other leading foreign currency at exactly the price prevailing for it against dollars when the word of the assassination first broke. All of this was possible, even though most of the foreign central banks had already closed for the weekend, because the Federal Reserve had established arrangements for activating its swaps with the other central banks up to the full amount of its existing lines with each. The result, of course, was that very little actual trading occurred. The potential strain was absorbed immediately because of the impressive evidence given that vast reserves were available—and that the United States was itself determined—to combat any bear raid on the dollar.

Standing behind these temporary facilities, designed for instantaneous use, are also the considerably larger resources of the IMF. The United Kingdom has, moreover, in four different sets of circumstances since World War II, gone to the IMF to draw. The United States, having for a long period been a supplier rather than a user of the IMF resources, made its first use of the IMF in an inconspicuous manner in the early years after the return of convertibility by simply reversing its previous role—the IMF began accumulating dollars instead of paying them out. But by the summer of 1963 the earlier United States creditor position was exhausted, and arrangments were made for it to begin to make actual drawings on the IMF.

Without going into details, it is important to realize that these arrangements, too, were specifically tailored to relieve another kind of potential strain on the dollar that arose from its reserve currency role. Other countries, accustomed to utilizing the dollar as a common means of payment, were no longer able to pay dollars directly into the IMF in paying off their past drawings, once the United States was no longer a creditor of the IMF. Under ordinary IMF procedures, they would have been required instead to convert those dollars into gold and then use the gold for payment to the IMF to reduce their own past drawings. But the United States, by going to the IMF to make drawings of its own, could match the amounts that other countries wished to repay in dollars. Currencies that the United States drew could be sold to the other countries in exchange for their dollars, and these other currencies in turn could then be used to repay the IMF. The need for the intermediate step of conversion into gold was eliminated. The consequent further drain of United States gold reserves was reduced by the full amount of the drawings made by the United States on the IMF—drawings which, after giving effect to various intervening uses of dollars, amounted to an outstanding total of about $300 million at the end of March 1965, and had reached a somewhat higher total in the autumn of 1964.

But in addition to this facility and other uses of IMF drawings to buttress the reserve currencies, there may also be a useful place for the granting of exceptional credits to the reserve currency countries by some of the other countries which, while in surplus position, are unable to provide the services of a reserve currency themselves. Proposals of this kind have taken various forms. One, most frequently mentioned with respect to the

United Kingdom, has been for a long-term loan to enlarge its monetary reserves, with amortization deferred for some years and eventual repayment completed after some ten, or fifteen, or possibly twenty years. Another suggestion, more often made concerning the United States, would be to absorb any overhang of short-term dollar holdings in official reserves by a "consolidation" through which other central banks would accept in exchange for a part of their present dollar reserves a long-term obligation of the United States, possibly denominated in their own currencies, in order to give contractual assurance against exchange risk. Indeed, the ground has been broken for such a possible approach, should it prove appropriate in the future, through the issuance over recent years by the U.S. Treasury of the special bonds denominated in the currency of the holders, although these bonds have customarily run for maturities in the neighborhood of only two years.

The design of these special bonds, and the questions that arose in their original issuance, brought into clear focus the fundamental problem that would have to be resolved before any substantial long-term credit could be extended by other central banks either to the United Kingdom or to the United States. That is, without regard to any question of the merits or lack of them in such an arrangement, the traditional requirements of central banks provide no room for illiquid long-term obligations. To be sure, should there be a spreading acceptance among central banks of the Italian method of reserve accounting, to which reference has already been made, there might be a place for loans of this kind in the second or third tier of central bank reserve assets. But even that would seem unlikely unless another step could also be taken. Means should be found to make the holdings of such a long-term obligation by any given central bank shiftable or redeemable or "bankable," on terms that would permit the obligation to qualify as an acceptable central bank asset.

The changes in monetary practices necessary to accomplish that purpose would indeed qualify as major reform. I shall come back to those in Chapter III. I should note, however, that an approach of this kind probably offers the most reasonable answer to the concern expressed by those who see a need for some way to make use of the large reserve holdings of countries that persist in maintaining surpluses—that is, the chronic surplus problem mentioned above.

5. *Can monetary reform systematize the creation of reserves?*

I have already suggested that there is little promise in any purely mechanical attempt to provide reserves automatically, with a regular percentage increase year by year. But I have left room for the implication that a managed creation of additional reserves might well be needed over the years ahead. The possibilities of accomplishing that through new methods of creating reserve assets will be left for the next chapter, but there are also some opportunities for achieving a greater degree of conscious control over the aggregate increase in reserves under present arrangements. Moreover, the experience of attempting to gauge the dimensions that such increases ought to reach might well be a useful precursor to any systematic effort to develop procedures for creating a new kind of reserve asset in the future.

With all the discussion of liquidity that has taken place in various official bodies, surprisingly little effort has been devoted to the hard practical problem of trying to determine what the increment in world-wide liquidity actually ought to be in relation to the various kinds of conditions influencing the need for liquidity, in the form of credit facilities as well as in the form of reserves. Effort has understandably focussed on techniques and on sweeping indictments of past shortcomings.

Clearly, the first step in determining an actual total for the appropriate increment to reserves at any particular time is to discover, on as current a basis as possible, what will be happening to reserves in any event. This requires a schedule of the other factors likely to be affecting international reserves, comparable to the schedules in familiar use for domestic purposes by the

Federal Reserve in this country, by the Bank of England for its domestic monetary control, and no doubt by other countries as well. That approach involves recent measurements, and projections for the period ahead, of each of the sources of domestic reserves and of each of the uses. The authorities then strike a balance in order to determine whether further official action is necessary to make an added increase, or a decrease, in the total reserves in order to bring them more nearly into line with policy judgments on what the evolution of reserves ought to be. Presumably any effort to introduce explicit determination of total reserves for the world economy would mean that some group somewhere must, in the pragmatic method of domestic central banking, review all other relevant factors of need and decide whether to add a little to, or subtract a little from, the flow of over-all reserve funds currently moving into place.

I am not going to try to work through such a hypothetical "factors analysis" here. Nor do I want to imply that the range of relevancy for changes in international reserves requires anything to compare with the frequency or the precision of the reserve calculations used within individual countries. But I do suggest that it is not too early for the staff of the IMF, or the Deputies of the Group of Ten, or Working Party 3, to begin attempting such exercises. And when they do, they will find there is still a long distance to be traveled before the various nations, even assuming they might have agreed on what they are against, can find sufficient common ground to agree on what they are "for." Once they decide, as I suspect they eventually may, that the appropriate level of precision requires only infrequent decisions to "add a little more," then I imagine they may also find that there are already several variables available, short of major reform, that might be used to try to carry through the marginal adjustments needed to bring the growth of world reserves on to "target," or into "target range."

Some of these can best be described in the next chapter, particularly those potentials of the IMF that merge into possibilites for reform. But to illustrate present possibilities, one technique would be merely to extend somewhat further the concept underlying the uses made of the IMF by the United States, a concept that was also embodied, at least in part, in handling the proceeds of the drawing from the IMF by the United Kingdom in 1961, and may have been under consideration in connection with its subsequent drawing in May 1965. That concept simply is so to arrange the currency content of IMF drawings as to absorb, or sterilize, or release, as appropriate, more or less of the reserve currencies themselves. The "bouquet" of currencies included in a drawing may include a very small amount of a reserve currency, for example, and include large amounts of the currencies of countries which have large dollar reserves. The drawing country may then exchange the other currencies for their dollars—using some, and holding some in reserves being accumulated as a demonstration of strength. There are, of course, a great variety of possible combinations. And in fulfillment of such objectives, the IMF might under its present Articles reach into new ground by initiating additional borrowing of strong currencies.

Such an approach is open to the risk of abuse, for a skeptic might argue that it would merely make the IMF a passive instrument for helping to absorb or release dollars in order to adjust the world-wide consequences of any deficits which the United States itself chose to go on incurring. However, I think I have already shown, or tried to show, that the recent "trial by ordeal" through which the United States has been passing, accompanied by the introduction of "multilateral surveillance," make this risk a comparatively slight one.

I would surely grant, however, that a precondition for the kind of testing that I am suggesting here is assurance that the United States will be capable of maintaining balance in its international accounts. And if the United States should incur a deficit for any of the usual reasons, there must be assurance that its approach to correction and the design of its transitional financing will be similar to that of other leading countries, and that the United States will expect to undergo the same kind of multilateral examination that other leading countries experience. If that can be granted, then there will be, in addition to the scope for maneuvers through the IMF, the whole range of possibilities already suggested through which the United States could take action on its own initiative—such as through the redemption of its own foreign currency bonds now outstanding or, even more importantly, through the acquisition of obligations issued by the governments or central banks of countries with strong currencies.

The issuance of added dollars in exchange for the currency of other countries would not, of course, affect the deficit of the United States on any system of balance-of-payments accounting. The acquisition of the liquid liabilities of foreign monetary authorities has for several years been recorded, quite properly, alongside gold acquisitions in the official statistics of the United States, as an offset to increasing short-term dollar liabilities. But in this process, the United States could acquire useful holdings of foreign currencies, while the world supply of dollars could be enlarged by a corresponding amount. Moreover, the fact that the United States would have other currencies which it could pay out, in lieu of gold, in the case of demands for gold from the countries whose currencies it held, would help to minimize the exposure of its gold reserve. That would be important. One of the grave risks to the system, in any substantial enlargement of the use of dollars as reserves, comes from the related drains this could place on the one gold reserve that now sustains the entire monetary system by assuring gold convertibility at a fixed price.

The problem in attempting to achieve some degree of conscious management of reserve balances (or of exerting a guiding influence upon their over-all changes) is not, I am sure, one of insufficient techniques, even under the system as it now exists. The difficult issues concern the extent to which the provision of primary liquidity should be left dependent upon the action of one country, and the way in which the questions of policy control can be resolved. These matters, as already noted, lead not only into the desire of other countries and international organizations to have a fuller voice, perhaps in concert, in the determination of the quantity of reserves, but also into the problem for the United States as to whether it should expect, as the principal supplier of reserve currencies, to bear the strains of continuing in this role if the determination of amounts is to be in a significant degree in the hands of others. Just as it may be argued that reserve creation is so important that all countries should be represented in determining the size and timing of substantial changes, so may it also be argued in reverse that such representation should carry with it an obligation to share in the burdens of reserve creation.

The Scope for Constructive Monetary Reform

It should now be clear that this book is not by any means intended to suggest discouragement over the present capabilities of the international monetary system. There are no economic needs that I can visualize for which facilities or potentialities within the system as it exists today are not at least minimally adequate, taking into account the innovations of the past few years. This is only to state, however, the minimum position. For it should also be clear by this time that I do agree with those who wish urgently to pursue the search for new methods of broadening and adding to the facilities now available.

The promising scope for additional reform lies in the development of new arrangements for creating some additional type of acceptable reserve asset. If that can be done, the use of any such new potential will require forthright resolution of the awesome obligation to develop some sort of standards for determining what the aggregate increase in international monetary reserves ought to be—standards that will be broadly acceptable to all countries. Beyond that, it will be necessary to place increased reliance upon international bodies for the appraisal of those standards or criteria in order to reach operational decisions quickly enough to be useful, and cautiously enough to avoid reckless excess, month by month or, more probably, year by year.

If ways can be seen toward achievement of these objectives, then the prerequisites should exist for the further elaboration of internationally available credit facilities through which increasing use can be made of any reserves already created. It would be as misguided internationally as it has long been proved to be domestically for anyone to assume that changes in money alone can be sufficient for the needs of a monetary system. Credit must always be recognized as the twin of money. The creation of reserves must always be paired with the development of credit facilities. These, together, are liquidity.

Multinational determination of some kind will presumably have to be made from time to time of the appropriate division between reliance upon credit facilities, with their built-in restraint upon overexpansion, and reliance upon outright reserves, with the greater degree of freedom they imply for autonomous national action. It will be important to find a place in this setting, too, for techniques that will permit the extending of credit by surplus countries to those countries whose currencies continue to serve both as vehicles for the private transactions of the world and, at least on some scale, as reserve currencies as well.

These are the areas of opportunity. What are the boundaries imposed upon them by the conditions for monetary order described in the first chapter? It seems to me they are the following:

1. Any new reserves that are introduced should be operationally interchangeable, at least by the monetary authorities of various countries, with any or all national currencies, whether those that are used only for domestic purposes within their own country, those used more widely as vehicle or trading currencies, or those used for reserve purposes.

2. New reserves should be either convertible directly into gold or made equivalent to gold through reliable undertakings by

those creating them—in order to retain the essential gold anchor of stability—and should be based on the established price of $35 per ounce.

3. New reserves, both in the method of their creation and in the range of their uses, should contribute to maintenance of the system of fixed parities for rates of exchange.

4. The creation of new reserves should be consistent with, and their patterns of use should help to reinforce, the maintenance of balance-of-payments discipline—that is, the maintenance of conditions in which nations are induced so to allocate their economic resources as to achieve viable balance in their relations with each other.

5. The holding and use of any new reserves should be subject to the free choice of individual sovereign nations and should not alter or disrupt any country's existing internal control over the issuance of its own currency.

6. New reserves should be consistent with the continued performance by the IMF of all its existing monetary and credit functions, and preferably should be usable by the IMF in making payments to its members or receiving payments from them.

7. New reserves should not interfere with the services performed by the vehicle currencies, whatever the scale these may reach, nor obstruct the continued use of reserve currencies by countries that choose to hold them, nor cast discredit on existing facilities or currencies that are in widespread use.

8. Any new credit facilities that may be established should conform to the conditions described for the creation of new reserves.

9. Confidence is essential for the survival of any monetary system. To assure the confidence of the banks, traders, and governments of the world and to gain acceptability for the new instruments or techniques, any new reserves and any new credit facilities should fit as closely as possible into familiar patterns of experience and assure the continuity of existing methods for making payments or employing balances.

These are the challenging conditions that should be recognized in any agenda for the future of the international monetary system. In the concluding chapter I shall try to indicate some of the possibilities that remain open, and some that may be excluded, if the system of the future is to remain consistent with these implications of the essential elements that I think must be preserved in the international monetary system.

III

AN AGENDA FOR
THE FUTURE

The Scope for Innovation

THE underlying problem that has been emerging for the international monetary system since the return of convertibility is not one of mere mechanics. As we have already seen, the system has in fact functioned remarkably well, providing for an unprecedented growth in the world's commerce. The deeper problem is whether, under the evolving conditions of convertibility, the monetary system can amply fulfill its potentials over the years ahead if the primary responsibility for supplying added reserves continues to rest upon a reserve currency created by one country.

In this chapter we shall be searching for ways in which other leading countries can share more fully in the provision of reserves. To be sure, some of the more recent innovations in international cooperation give many of these other countries a clearer role in influencing the course followed by the United States itself, through which added dollars are contributed to the reserve base of the monetary system. But that first step should be accompanied by some pairing of the privilege of participation in "surveillance" with the responsibility for providing resources. Modest forward steps have been made in this respect, too, as the quotas of some of these countries in the International Monetary Fund have increased proportionately more than the average, and as several have participated in the arrangements for special lending to the IMF initiated by the Group of Ten.

Much more can and should be done through increasing IMF

quotas or through lending to the IMF in the future, and I shall come back to those possibilities later in this chapter; but the area that most needs to be probed in exploring the potentials for major innovation is that of creating additional reserve assets through group action. However that is done, as I have already stressed, such assets should be designed to be acceptable to the monetary authorities of all countries, and be readily interchangeable by them with their national currencies and with any vehicle currencies currently in widespread use. Such an asset should presumably also be defined in terms of gold at the same $35 fixed price that now prevails—and maintained there if the workings of Gresham's Law are not to be set loose upon an international scale. Moreover, in whatever form the additional asset is introduced, it should allow room for other kinds of growth and diversification within the international monetary system. It should not preclude, for example, the ultimate appearance of a common currency for the Common Market, which might at some future time take its place alongside the dollar, and possibly sterling, as an important vehicle currency.

There may well be room, of course, for more than one kind of additional reserve asset. The type most commonly visualized would be a primary reserve asset, with a standing comparable to that of the dollar in being considered "as good as gold." Conceivably, there is also room for a second type of reserve asset, one which might be considered secondary in form. A long-term loan for the purposes of increasing the reserves of a leading country could fill this role for the lending countries, if the debt instrument were so designed as to make it possible for other central banks, having advanced the funds, to then treat the instrument as a suitable asset for their own holdings.

Nor is there any reason to expect that either the primary or the secondary type of reserve asset should come into being all at once with all its characteristics fully agreed upon and all countries committed to its use. Just as a number of the steps already taken in international cooperation have been providing experience along the way toward the possible creation of new reserve assets, so the further steps taken in the actual process of creating such assets can be regarded as evolutionary. This chapter will consequently be devoted, first, to a survey of some of the possible initial conditions for, and characteristics of, a newly created primary reserve asset; second, to some of the attributes that might at least originally be appropriate for an acceptable secondary reserve asset; and third, to a sketch of the possibilities for harmonizing the old and the new through action that might be considered over, say, the next three or four years, and also to a few strokes across the canvas of the more distant future.

Creating a Primary Reserve Asset

Scores of suggestions have been made for the technical design of a new reserve unit. Disputation has been both lengthy and agitated among the various proponents. Yet, although those debates have been helpful in clarifying the range of possibilities, they have at this early stage probably diverted undue effort and attention to details of mechanics, away from the crucial issues of principle that must be faced before meaningful action can be initiated toward the creation of any new reserve asset.

In my own view, there is relatively little to choose among the various contrivances that have been suggested over recent years, once they have been tailored to fit certain necessary or desirable conditions which will be described shortly. An open receptivity as to the techniques does not prevent me from indicating some preferences in the pages which follow. But whether or not those particular suggestions are accepted is relatively unimportant. The detailed questions of technique can be resolved fairly readily in the usual give-and-take of international negotiation, once there has been agreement on the fundamental "constitutional" questions:

—Where should the new unit be created?
—Who will contribute to the new unit, and in what proportions?

—Who will receive the original distribution of the new unit?
—Who will be permitted to make use of it, once issued?
—Who will decide upon the amounts of the new unit to be created from time to time, and how will those decisions be reached?

These various questions can best be discussed individually, with the suggested answers building step by step toward an outline of an over-all approach. For that reason, I only attempt here the barest outline of some of the possibilities, by way of introduction, and shall draw together the various segments of the whole in a somewhat more systematic way later on.

It is not my intention to introduce another full-blown plan into the collection with which the literature on the international monetary system already abounds, nor to become an ardent advocate of any specific recommendations. My suggestions are intended only as loosely connected ideas, reasonably interrelated and, hopefully, mutually consistent. They center on the issues of principle that will have to be resolved before direction can be given to the much more detailed effort needed for the formulation of any concrete plan. They will serve their purpose if they highlight the issues in a meaningful and provocative way.

1. *An introductory sketch of some possibilities.*

It seems to me that any new reserve asset should be created within the IMF, and I would suggest setting up what might be called a "Fund Unit Account." Individual countries would contribute their own currencies to the Account. Countries would qualify to contribute by virtue of the uses already being made of their currencies, either as reserve currencies or through drawings of their currencies from the IMF. The proportionate shares of each country in these contributions would be determined by taking into consideration the extent to which their currencies had been used for these other international purposes over recent years. The total amount to be created at any time would be determined in a two-stage process: first, a recommendation would be voted by a small group of IMF Governors representing both contributing and noncontributing countries; and second, final action would be taken by a vote of all IMF Governors.

Once allocated a potential contributing share, each country would be free to make all, or part, or none of the contribution; any shortfall would be reallocated among the other contributors. Shares would be determined anew, and countries would individually decide on their further participation at the time of each new increment to the Fund Unit Account. In turn, each contributing country would receive a corresponding "checking account deposit" in the Fund Unit Account. This it could spend, lend, invest, or use to make grants, at its own discretion, through payments to other monetary authorities or international financial institutions. The currencies deposited in the Account would remain in the Account. They would only be paid out to reduce the total of Fund Units or to dissolve the arrangement.

In return for having acquired a usable reserve asset by simply issuing some of its own obligations to the Fund Unit Account—that is, as a condition for being a creator of reserve assets—each contributing country would accept certain obligations. It would agree to maintain the original gold value of any installment of its own currency contributed to the Account. After receiving its allocations of Fund Units and paying out some or all of them, it would agree to accept Fund Units subsequently from any other monetary authority or international financial institution at least up to the accumulated amount of its own original contributions to the Account. And it would agree to maintain the external convertibility of its own currency through the purchase and sale of gold at a fixed price appropriately related to the established price of $35 per ounce.

Within this context progress might be expected to occur toward a gradual evening out of gold reserve ratios among leading countries, without the necessity of specific agreement on a uniform percentage for all countries. Reserve currencies would be supplemented but not supplanted. The new Fund Units themselves would only be held by and exchanged among monetary authorities or official international financial institutions. Although none but the contributors would be required to hold the Units, this assured lodgment should make the Units generally acceptable to others. Vehicle currencies would continue to be used for all of the regular needs of commerce; monetary authorities could use Fund Units to obtain needed amounts of vehicle currencies from each other.

This, to be sure, is an idealized and unduly simplified rendering of a number of very complex matters. As a schematic diagram it may, however, prove helpful as an introductory guide into the responses that I am about to suggest to the various questions already posed concerning the fundamentals of any new arrangements.

2. *Where should the new unit be created?*

The further evolution of the international monetary system should be toward closer integration among the participant currencies, rather than toward fragmentation. Consequently, instead of creating a new entity for the management and issuance of any newly created reserve asset, the world should find a way to make use of the facilities already in existence for the exercise of multilateral responsibility in the international monetary system—specifically the IMF. Inevitably, many arrangements will be proposed, even including wide variations among the possibilities suggested for action inside the IMF, in answer to the other questions soon to be discussed; but there is an overriding need to resolve, first, the question of "where should the asset be created" in favor of the IMF itself.

While the actual contributions toward a new reserve asset will have to come from countries whose resources permit them to commit significant amounts, there would only be an exacerbation of the divisive criticism that the role of the dollar has already aroused if the next step were to be the deliberate establishment of a new body to provide reserve facilities that consisted of only a small group of countries creating reserves for their own exclusive use. If there is to be a further contribution of liquidity in the form of another approach to the creation of reserve assets, the only satisfactory location for that function is alongside the most comprehensive international arrangements already engaged in the allocation of credit facilities for monetary purposes —that is, alongside the present operations of the IMF.

In the earliest stages in the evolution of central banks for national economies, it was found useful to establish two parallel functions: those of a "banking department" and those of an "issue department." In effect, the IMF now is, by analogy, a "banking department." What I am urging is that a new entity be established within the IMF for the distinct purpose of creating monetary reserves; in other words, the establishment of an "issue department."

The political reasons are obvious enough for seeking identification between any powerful new force for the conscious creation of a monetary reserve asset and the one monetary organization already in being which represents all countries (and to which all countries can belong on fulfilling uniform qualifying requirements). There are also, of course, mechanical advantages. But more important than any of these, there must be a basis for confidence in whatever new facility is introduced. The IMF has in twenty years of operation, established a basis for confidence that no new entity could possibly duplicate.

3. *Who is to contribute, and in what proportions?*

The criteria for selecting countries to participate in the creation of new reserve assets should, if at all possible, be self-qualifying and self-enforcing. That is the way in which sterling, and later the dollar, moved into their roles both as vehicle and as reserve currencies. There must also be a ready willingness of the eligible countries to participate. Indeed, the rejection by all other countries of any possible use of their own currencies, on an individual basis, as reserve currencies accounts for the widespread tacit agreement that any new steps in the future will have to be taken on a group basis.[1]

[1] See Appendix, paragraph 25c.

Presumably the new unit, however it comes to be denominated, will be formed by the contribution of various national currencies. Three rather simple criteria for self-qualifying selection may suffice. One is that any country whose currency has already been used for international reserve purposes should be qualified—if it wishes to do so, and if it meets the two other qualifications—to place an amount of its own currency in the common pool or Account for a new reserve asset administered by the IMF. That is, not only countries whose currencies are directly in active use for reserve purposes, but also countries whose currencies have been used in drawing at the IMF, should be eligible. Presumably the measurement of use, subject to general qualifications to be suggested below, should be on a gross basis. The second requirement would be that each contributing country, in order to provide the essential link with gold, should be prepared to undertake to maintain the gold-dollar value of its contribution to the Account just as it does with respect to its IMF commitments. That is, if it should for any reason devalue, it should "pay-up" an additional amount of its own currency to fully offset the decline in the value of the amount already contributed to the Account. The third condition should be that any contributing country commit itself to accept from other monetary authorities, and hold at any time, an amount of Fund Units equal to its own accumulated contributions.

There would, of course, be a risk that countries might wish, perhaps merely for prestige reasons, to achieve participating status by arranging to have token amounts of their own currencies drawn from the IMF. In order to assure a bona fide standard of calculation, there might have to be agreement on some minimum level of use. For example, to become eligible for a contributing membership in the new currency arrangements a given country might be required to account for, say, at least 1 per cent of the total drawings made from the IMF over the five preceding calendar years. In this way, of course, some further impetus would be given to encouraging countries while in surplus or strong positions to acquiesce in the active use of their currencies by the IMF management in meeting its ordinary drawing requirements. Use of a period of five years, or possibly even longer, to determine that significant use was being made of a currency would be desirable in order to avoid frequent shifts of one country or another from eligible to ineligible status simply because it happened itself to be a net debtor of the IMF from time to time.

Once the threshold problem is resolved—that is, which countries are eligible to share in the creation of the new reserve asset —the related important question is that of deciding upon proportionate shares. It is certainly possible that determination of the proportion which each country would contribute to the total in the new currency Account year by year could be resolved on some basis related to the same criterion for participation, namely, the extent to which each currency has been used for international reserve purposes. Eligible countries might contribute their own currencies in any given accounting period to provide a given increment of Fund Units according to an agreed basis which gave great weight to the ratio between the use made of each currency over, say, the preceding five years and the total use made of all currencies over those years, both as reserve currencies and through drawings from the IMF. It would not be sufficient for determining proportionate shares to leave the measurement solely in terms of currencies drawn from the IMF over the preceding period. There should, it would appear, be at least a comparable provision made for the additional uses of reserve currencies over the same relevant base period. If the volume of outstanding official accounts held in dollars should have gone up on average over the preceding five years, for example, then weight should be given to that alongside the average annual drawings of dollars and other currencies from the IMF.

Details of this kind are always resolved more effectively in the full light of the considerations evoked by actual negotiation. There is no need to attempt here to do more than indicate the lines of possible approach. And those lines, as I see it, need merely be that eligibility for participation would be determined by the fact that a given currency had reached sufficient strength and acceptability to have been used by other countries on a significant scale, either directly or through drawings on the IMF, and that proportionate contributions to a new currency pool might, whenever new increments are made, be determined by taking into account the relative extent to which use has recently been made of the various currencies eligible for participation. There are, to be sure, a host of other possible criteria for influencing the shares of individual countries that the IMF has already developed for use in determining the distribution of the IMF's present quotas among countries. It is no criticism of those standards for that purpose to suggest that another standard—recent use for international monetary purposes—be given considerable weight in determining the shares of contributing countries in a new Fund Unit.

While no country should be able to contribute more than its proportionate share, however that proportion were to be determined from year to year, each country should as an attribute of its own sovereignty be permitted to contribute less, or not at all. It would follow from the permissive nature of this arrangement that any agreement on a total of the added reserve asset to be created at any given time should not be nullified by the decision of one country or another to contribute less or not at all, but that there shoud be a rearrangement of total shares, following the same principles of proportionality, in order to achieve the predetermined total. This kind of flexible arrangement is not completely unknown to the leading countries. In fact, this is very much the pattern that has been followed in the informal arrangements through which eight of these countries have pooled their contributions of gold to meet net drains from the London gold market, and have also at times readjusted among themselves the distribution of net gold proceeds, as these accrued to the gold pool from its operations in the London gold market.

There is one other qualification that probably ought to be considered in determining the amounts that would be entered for each country in any general calculation of proportionate shares.

It would not seem appropriate for this purpose to include among the uses of a given currency any special acquisitions made of that currency by the IMF through selling gold to the particular country. In the same way, in calculating any increase in the average use of a particular currency as a reserve currency, there should be a deduction of increases in the gold holdings of a reserve currency country from any average increase computed in the reserve balances held in that country by other countries. Whether or not the converse should apply, with a country such as the United States receiving "credit" for its gold outpayments, is not clear, except possibly when the country is losing gold while in a surplus position in its balance of payments.

The principle, at any rate, is clear. Countries would in fact participate in the creation of an additional reserve asset on terms that reflected the net contribution that the currencies of each had already made over the preceding base period to world liquidity—through drawings of that currency from the IMF's regular holdings; through drawings of that currency made possible because the IMF had, in turn, borrowed additional amounts of that currency from its issuing central bank; and through the net increase in official holdings of any particular currency, that is, in the uses made of it as a reserve currency.[2] (It is possible that allowance might be made for the actual use of currencies under activated swaps as well, but the temporary nature of such facilities might argue against including them in the base

[2] These generalizations are not intended to imply an exclusion of Switzerland. The fact that Switzerland is not a member of the IMF means that it would have to be given a special status in any Account formed for the creation of an additional reserve asset, should the Swiss themselves wish to qualify for participation. One criterion could, of course, be the extent to which Swiss francs were used, on average, for supplemental reserve loans made in parallel with the lending activities of the Group of Ten. Switzerland has made two such loans in connection with the Group of Ten credits to the IMF for transfer to the United Kingdom in November 1964 and May 1965, for example. It is strongly to be hoped, of course, that Switzerland will in any event soon follow the implications of its growing role in the world's monetary system to their ultimate conclusion by joining the IMF as a full member.

for calculating the net use of various currencies. This is typical of the questions that should be resolved through intergovernmental negotiation, possibly as reviewed in the light of recent developments whenever a new increment to Fund Units was being made.)

The dependence of the new reserve asset upon contributions of individual currencies would, of course, raise serious doubts in the minds of many who realize that the record of most currencies, even of those of some of the leading countries, has been very irregular. In terms of equivalent gold content, following the general wave of currency adjustments in the 1930s, the deterioration in all currencies except the dollar has been striking. On a percentage scale, in relation to 1934, while the dollar remains at 100, the French franc works out, for example, at 3 per cent, the German mark at 4 per cent, and the Belgian franc at 9 per cent; although the Dutch guilder and the Swiss franc have held close to 40 per cent and 70 per cent, respectively. Against this record, not even a recent period of strength over four or five years is likely to be completely persuasive to a world that demands a currency system founded on confidence.

A compelling case might be made, therefore, for one additional criterion which any individual country should meet in order to qualify as a participant in the creation of an additional reserve asset. There would be much less doubt concerning the determination of any participating country to maintain the gold value of its own currency if each would undertake, as the United States has done for so long, to buy and sell gold at a par value corresponding to the implied gold content of the parity for its currency that it has declared to the IMF. The pressure of potential gold withdrawals, in the event of undue inflationary developments within any of the contributing countries, would help to assure that steps would be taken by that country to keep the value of its currency from depreciating further. Such protection would be a useful defense against an erosion of the value of a currency included in the Fund Unit, short of the condition of actual devaluation for which the maintenance of the gold-value provision itself would provide protection.

In view of the very large holdings of gold that have been accumulated by several of the European countries, with the total of European gold holdings now much larger than those of the United States, there should be no practical obstacle to commitments of this kind. Moreover, implicit support of this view was offered as well by the Finance Minister of France, when outlining his government's approach to French gold policy in February 1965. He stated then that France readily acknowledged the two-way nature of its gold acquisitions—i.e., that it should expect to sell as well as to buy.[3] Acceptance of an obligation to buy or sell gold at parity, on the part of the participating countries, might well be a prerequisite to the agreement of the United States to participate. Without a generalized commitment of this kind, waves of world-wide unrest—when they occur, as they always will—could lead to an undue convergence of demand for gold upon the U.S. gold reserves.

4. *Who will receive the original distribution, and in what proportions?*

Any new unit must, as I have been suggesting, be built upon contributions of national currencies. Its credibility as a wholly new, and unknown, unit of account will depend upon the assured integrity of those national contributions and upon the readiness with which such a Fund Unit can actually be used by central banks in making settlements with each other. Because of its nature as a composite unit, it will not be usable in the foreign-exchange markets for trading against national currencies, at least not for a long time until habits and mores have developed around it. Perhaps, as will be mentioned below, there will even have to be an early phase during the initial transition to the use of pooled resources in reserves in which the grouping of the currencies might instead be identified with the dollar, rather than

[3] M. Valéry Giscard d'Estaing, *Lecture on the International Monetary System*, Ambassade de France, Speeches and Press Conferences no. 218, February 11, 1965.

with a wholly new unit, in order to gain acceptance among the countries which do not contribute to the Account. (That would simply mean the issuance of dollars against a pool of foreign currencies held by the United States.) In any event, however, once a Fund Unit is established, it is a virtually inevitable consequence of the elements of double entry bookkeeping that the original distribution of the new units (that is, the "checking account" claims on the Fund Unit Account) will have to be made to the countries whose currencies are contributed to the Account.

Unless all of the contributing countries are prepared to make all or part of their original contribution as an outright gift, they will have to acquire some form of asset in exchange for the transfer to the Account of their own currency. Nor is there any need to burden a new mechanism with the additional problems of obtaining legislative approval at home for an outright gift. All that should be needed is legislative authorization for each contributing country to exchange an amount of its own obligations, denominated in its own currency, for a new kind of asset. The contributing countries should obtain in the original distribution a number of Fund Units corresponding exactly with the proportion of their own currency contribution to the total.

The process should not stop there. The Fund Unit Account itself should retain all of the currencies paid into it, and receive an agreed interest return on each of them from the issuing countries, for reasons to be described shortly. But the contributing countries would surely in turn expect to make active use of their proceeds. Acquisition of usable reserves, for general and widespread use in making transfers to other monetary authorities, would indeed be a strong inducement urging the eligible participants to accept the full measure of shares allotted to them. Some, of course, might currently have a clear need to restore their own reserves or have deficits to finance, but in general they would presumably wish to spend, lend, invest, or give away their own allocations of the new Fund Unit within some reasonable period of time. It would also be possible to design arrangements through which countries could, if they wished, transfer their Fund Units to the IMF itself, which, acting in its present normal capacity, could simply borrow the Units and in turn use them for any purposes approved by the Executive Directors.

The desire of the contributing countries to use their newly acquired assets would assure that the new Fund Units would eventually pass into general use among the monetary authorities of all countries. Yet each contributing country would have made its own determination of the initial use which it wished to make of its own share of this new asset. The later recipients of the new liquidity, as it was distributed by the original contributors, would have earned what they gained, or would have qualified for receiving the Units as aid in accordance with standards deemed adequate by the granting country. There would be no need for an international body to determine where or how to spend the assets contributed to the Account, although any contributing country which wished to put the shares it had received into the International Bank for Reconstruction and Development, for example, for use there, should be free to do so. There would be none of the risks, however, of an automatic or built-in linkage between the instrumentality for the creation of reserve assets and the quite separate matter of providing development aid to the less developed countries.

The integrity of the Fund Unit itself would be assured by the Fund's retention of all the currencies paid in, buttressed by the "maintenance of value" clause for the event of devaluation by any contributing currency and by the agreement of the contributing countries to hold at any time amounts up to the total of their own contributions. Moreover, if there were ever a decision to shrink total liquidity by contracting these reserves, the Fund Unit management could readily accomplish that by paying back to each contributor the indicated pro rata amount of its own currency, and by extinguishing a corresponding amount of the Fund Units that each of the contributing countries held, or might obtain.

The Fund Unit would not accomplish a meaningful net increase in liquidity, to be sure, or a corresponding increase in world commerce, if the contributing countries merely added their new claims to the other reserve assets which they already held. That is, the contributing countries could neutralize an intended increase in total reserves for the world at large by merely adding an equivalent amount of the new Units, or of other reserve assets, to the totals already in their own reserves. But if leading countries, once committed to a major new effort to generate liquid reserves for general use, decide instead on their own initiative to frustrate the objective, there is no way consistent with the retention of national sovereignty to compel any other result under any system. There would, however, be the continuing procedures of multilateral surveillance to help persuade a recalcitrant member to comply in practice with the intent.

Care would be necessary, moreover, to avoid a premature judgment that any contributing country was frustrating the intended expansion. For in the normal evolution of trade, some of the contributing members in any given year would be in overall surplus, presumably acquiring Fund Units as a part of the settlements received from others. Appropriate surveillance would itself require a full analysis of each country's position in the way that recently established arrangements already make quite practicable. While such an analysis could not depend upon a mere finding that a contributing country had failed to reduce its holdings of Fund Units by the full amount of its recent contribution to the Account, the prospect of searching group criticism would of itself be a strong force impelling a bona fide constructive use of the new resources by any contributing country. One way to view the situation is to realize that initial acquisition of Fund Units would, assuming all of a country's other accounts were in balance, be equivalent to putting it in a surplus position, in which case the country should take steps to bring its position back toward balance. Corresponding implications could be derived for other kinds of initial positions.

And, at the worst, if one or another country did decide to "go it alone" and merely hold for itself, as a further enlargement of its own reserves, the proceeds in Fund Units resulting from its own contributions, the arrangements as a whole would still go forward. The individual country, by impounding for itself the reserves it had acquired as part of the new liquidity creation, would have affected only its own contribution. Presumably, any agreed criteria for the qualifications of contributors would also provide for the eventual disqualification, for further participation, of a country found to be persistently neutralizing the intended effect or usefulness of its own contribution without good cause.

Perhaps these suggestions would become clearer if some of them were briefly restated in terms of what the arrangements mentioned thus far might mean for the United States. The indicated amount of its own contribution to a Fund Unit Account would be determined, under international voting procedures not yet described, on a basis that gave considerable weight to the average annual increase in the dollar balances of foreign central banks over some recent period of years, say five, and the average annual use of dollars in regular drawings from the IMF over that period. Committees of experts would have had to spend many months negotiating the accepted details of measurement— to determine which measurements were statistical aberrations that should not be counted, and which uses were in effect more than offset by repayments or by drawings which the United States had made itself—but all that we can by-pass for the present.

The important points are the following:

1. The United States would have participated in a determination that a certain amount of new Fund Units should be created —on that I shall say more very shortly.

2. The management of the Fund Unit Account would, according to an agreed formula and procedure, have worked out the proportion of this total that the United States was entitled to contribute in terms reflecting the uses that the rest of the world had been making of dollars, for various official purposes, in the recent past.

3. The United States could contribute all, or part, or none of this amount, as it decided; but any part which it chose not to contribute would be reallocated among the other contributing countries as an increase in their contributions, and would correspondingly result in an increase in their reserves available for general use.

4. In return for its contribution, which it would probably make to the Fund Unit Account in special issues of Treasury notes bearing interest as internationally agreed, the United States would receive a corresponding allocation of Fund Units which it would transfer to central banks or international financial institutions to meet net drains resulting from making purchases anywhere abroad, or from making foreign loans, or from acquiring foreign investments, or from making grants to less developed countries. The receiving countries would in turn have earned, or qualified for receiving, these added reserve assets by meeting the normal criteria and well-understood standards for commerce between individual countries.

Perhaps a comment should be added on interest payments, and on why it seems to me that interest should be payable on the currencies put into the Fund Unit Account by each contributing country, although no interest should be paid by the Account in turn to holders of Fund Units. The contributors should expect to pay interest because, in return for placing their own national obligations in the Account, they would receive usable Fund Units which they could employ in meeting their own external commitments. They would have, in effect, borrowed in their own currency to obtain an internationally usable asset. The original recipients and the subsequent users of Fund Units should not expect to receive interest, however, because they would have acquired an asset designed to be an internationally guaranteed equivalent to gold. While the guaranty would not run from the Fund Unit Account to the holder of Fund Units, there would be a guaranty by each contributor to the IMF, assuring that the amount of each contributed currency would have its original gold value maintained within the Fund Unit Account.

Presumably, the interest paid by the contributors should be relatively low because of the other obligations undertaken by the contributors as participants. Subject to periodic review through the established management machinery, a rate of, say, 3 per cent might be appropriate under conditions comparable to those of 1965. This would assure that eligible countries would have to make some annual payment for the privilege of issuing their own obligations, in effect, as reserve assets. The interest payments to the Fund Unit Account should provide a sufficient income to the IMF to cover all administrative expenses and permit a modest annual transfer to a surplus account. In time, the surplus could become a cushion for absorbing any possible losses through outright default on the part of any contributing country.

The nonpayment of interest to users of the Unit would be consistent with its status as purely a reserve asset. It would only be held in monetary reserves or in international financial institutions and would not be usable for trading in the foreign-exchange markets of the world. Thus it would have to be exchanged for a vehicle currency to be used directly for trading or investment purposes. Any vehicle currency, then as now, would bear interest as determined by the flow of supply and demand forces among the various markets where it was in actual use. In short, a complementary, and not a competitive, relationship would exist between the Fund Unit and the dollar, for example.

Nor need there necessarily be concern that the reserves of the United States would become filled with Fund Units, paid in by other countries seeking dollars or gold. For the Fund Units would, or should, within a short time acquire a respect and standing comparable to gold, as a reserve asset, because of the obligations of the contributing countries to maintain the gold value of their contributions to the Fund Unit Account. Those obligations would be reinforced, against the outside risk of revolution and abrogation, by the accumulation of the surplus in the Fund Unit Account.

At the same time, however, the Fund Units would be similar to other claims on the IMF in that they could not be used directly in the trade marts, but would have to be converted into vehicle currencies or other usable national currencies to pass over into the normal and accustomed channels of banking and business. In this way, as in others, assurance would be provided against any undue rivalry with the dollar, for example. There would be no discredit cast upon the dollar by this kind of reserve supplement, and no reason to fear a shrinkage of liquidity through a disappearance of dollars from the uses which they now fulfill.

Moreover, so long as all contributing countries also accepted a parallel obligation to sell as well as to buy gold at the equivalent of parity for their own currency, there would be no more reason for a convergence of demand for gold upon the United States than upon any other contributing country. The recent pattern—in which gold on leaving the United States virtually disappeared from general accessibility in the international monetary system—should itself disappear under the conditions of mutual responsibility and mutual reinforcement for the system that would be contemplated by the establishment of a Fund Unit. In effect, the gold reserves of all of the contributing countries would become available to meet runs occurring on any one of them, so long as that one country was not itself in an extreme and persistent deficit position (and thus unable to purchase gold from others to help meet its own losses). And over time, as countries gained confidence in the continuance of these arrangements, a gradual process of redistribution of gold holdings would probably begin, working toward the patterns of compatability in gold ratios that several leading governors of central banks have, quite appropriately, been calling for over the past few years.[4]

The array of possible uses, and some of the problems in getting Fund Units activated, deserve a closer look.

[4] See also Appendix, paragraph 38.

5. *Who will use the new unit, and how?*

To continue the specific illustration concerning the United States, most probably the Treasury would set up accounts for the Fund Units that would parallel its monetary gold account. Official accounting for reserve assets would include these Units, along with any holdings of convertible foreign currencies by the Treasury or the Federal Reserve. But as with its gold, the Treasury would presumably use the Fund Units, at least for some years, only to make official settlements with other countries or international organizations. The difference would be that any Fund Units received on original issue from the Fund Unit Account, or an equivalent amount of such units, would ordinarily be expected to flow out over some reasonable period as a result of increased imports, or paying past debts, or an increased granting of credits, or increased investment, or increased aid. Partly because of its vehicle currency role, however, the United States should continue to expect substantial two-way flows of Fund Units through its accounts.

The United States might conceivably use the Fund Units, as it could gold, to buy other currencies from their issuing central banks, and in turn sell these currencies to American firms in need of such currencies to make payments abroad. Or it could sell the Fund Units directly to foreign central banks in exchange for dollars which those central banks had been accumulating. Or it could lend the Fund Units to the IMF or use them to make a contribution or payment to the International Bank for Reconstruction and Development, for example, or to the Inter-American Development Bank. Or if appropriate arrangements could be agreed upon by the IMF, it might use the Fund Units to repay an ordinary drawing from the IMF itself, just as the IMF might also want to consider using Fund Units to meet some of its drawings.

In turn, the United States could acquire Fund Units by transferring dollars to central banks which wished to obtain a vehicle currency for actual use in exchange for some of their Fund Unit holdings. Or it could receive Fund Units in the same way that gold payments now flow to the United States, and for the same purposes.

While only illustrative, these possibilities suggest certain lines of usage that would most likely prevail for some years until further changes in the international environment necessitated another "new look" at the international monetary system. The Fund Units would not pass directly into the foreign-exchange markets; would not be held by private traders and bankers; but would, when transferred to any particular monetary authority, increase its own inner reserves and enable it to free for sale to its own banks, or in the foreign-exchange market, some of its holdings of any currency then actively in use as a vehicle currency.

The Fund Unit would be exchangeable at any central bank for its own currency, provided the central bank itself was willing, at an indicated rate of exchange fixed by the IMF in terms of the declared par values of the leading countries. The contributing countries would, as already mentioned, receive Fund Units against their own currency. And since each contributing country would also undertake to buy and sell gold at parity, any central bank holder of Fund Units could, through successive conversions, turn the Fund Units into gold if it wished to do so. Presumably, arrangements could also be considered in the IMF for enabling the Fund Unit to be pledged as collateral for an automatic borrowing of any specific currency from the IMF, and for enabling it to be used in lieu of gold by countries making the gold tranche contribution of a quota subscription. The full array of arrangements, if found acceptable by enough countries, should indeed provide adequately, in present conditions, for the sharing of a significant proportion of the reserve currency responsibilities, and opportunities, among countries that have become able to share them.

The monetary authorities of every country, or at least every member of the IMF, would thus be free to acquire and use the Fund Units in their own reserves, in payments to other monetary authorities, and in payments to international financial institutions. The fact that lodgment of the full amount outstanding could always be assured by the readiness of all contributors to acquire Fund Units equal to their own contributions should give the Units a general acceptability among all monetary authorities. Assuming that the questions of decision-making authority can be resolved, the Fund Units could then represent a new element in, and add new dimension to, the supply of reserves available to the international monetary system. Against this background, it becomes possible to take a meaningful look at the possibilities of establishing principles for the decision-making process.

6. *Who will decide upon the amounts, and how?*

The functions of management of a Fund Unit Account could be readily delegated to the Managing Director and staff of the IMF, operating in conformity with the general rules and specific decisions reached in the Executive Board. But the crucial decisions as to the amount and timing of actual changes in the quantity of Fund Units outstanding would have to be made—as the decisions on IMF quotas are made—at the level of Governors, i.e., the finance ministers and central bank governors who can speak for the member countries as principals. It is on these questions of representation and of the possible infringement of sovereignty, as the amount and extent of national commitments were to be determined, that all proposals for international monetary reform have encountered their gravest difficulty.

The suggestions made thus far have all been conditioned by respect for the necessities of sovereignty, particularly as these have become embodied in those lasting elements of the present international monetary system which were noted in the first chapter:

1. National currencies would continue in exclusive use within individual countries, and control over their issuance would always be a matter of national sovereignty.

2. A very few currencies of leading countries would continue to be used as vehicle currencies for the international needs of bankers and traders, although the total amounts outstanding would still be determined by their own national monetary authorities.

3. Some vehicle currencies would also continue to be used as reserve currencies, at least on the scale presently reached.

4. Any other element of reserves would have to be interchangeable with the currencies already in use in the three sectors of the international system—the national, the vehicle, and the reserve; or more broadly, individual countries must retain freedom of choice over the disposition of their reserves.

5. Most countries will be members of the IMF and able to use its credit facilities, as well as credit obtainable from individual countries or groups of countries, in financing some part of their individual reserve needs through corrective periods of balance-of-payments adjustment.

Moreover, so far as actual contributions for the creation of a new unit are concerned, the suggestions made thus far have been solely in terms of a pool formed of existing national currencies. There would be self-qualifying standards of eligibility, based upon the past performance of the particular currencies. No country would, however, be compelled to pay in its currency, even if eligible. Yet, once it had elected to contribute for a given installment, a country could not negate its pledge for that amount. Should it devalue, for example, it would be required to make a compensating further payment into the Account. Should it wish to withdraw its contributions, once made, that would presumably be subject to some general action by the contributing group as a whole.

These conditions to be met by the contributing countries would merely reflect the carrying through of specific agreements solemnly undertaken, increment by increment, as additions came to be made to the Fund Unit Account, and not a generalized surrender of sovereignty for the future. Once it had received the new unit, a contributing country would ordinarily be expected to use it by employing the proceeds it had received from what had been, in effect, a permanent loan which it had just placed with the new Account—but as this would only be an implied obligation, it would not be compulsory.

Despite these and other precautions already noted in the greater detail of my earlier comments, the hard question still remains—by whom, and how, can the crucial decisions be reached? Some of the decisions are essentially constitutional and long-range, to be made at the start and then reviewed only at rather long intervals. These, embodied in the acceptance of an original charter or mandate, might well have to be ratified by the same majority of member countries in the IMF that is required for an amendment to its present Articles. But included in this originating mandate would be a provision determining the procedure for reaching each operational decision to increase or decrease the supply of Fund Units outstanding. That is the procedure which I would like to discuss now.

The obvious suggestion, often volunteered by countries which might expect to be contributors to one or another of the various liquidity plans and thus rightly concerned that they should not obligate themselves for too much, has been that a number of leading countries should form a group of their own to make this decision and carry it out. Another, equally obvious suggestion has come from countries most concerned over the possibility of a chronic shortage of world liquidity. Their proposal is to let the IMF decide, perhaps by simple majority under the present weighted voting system. Most of the better-known reform proposals have leaned toward some version of the second approach partly because, for reasons already mentioned, the creation of added liquidity is too important a matter, for world politics as well as for world economics, to be left to any smaller group than that which, as nearly as any group can, represents all countries.

Perhaps there is a possibility of reconciliation between these extremes by drawing a distinction between initiation and approval, along lines roughly analogous to the procedure already followed by the Group of Ten in connection with the activation of the General Arrangements to Borrow. Any change, up or down, could be first broached by the Managing Director of the IMF, or by a new special committee of Governors, to which I will refer here for convenience as the Governors' Committee on Fund Units. By whomever started, the proposal would not attain action status until it had been formally reviewed and formulated as a specific recommendation by the Governors' Committee on Fund Units. The recommendation could then, in turn, be presented at the Annual Meeting to all the IMF Governors for debate, and approval or rejection. Action might require perhaps a two-thirds vote, weighted by existing quotas; and the tenor of the debate would, of course, condition the nature of further recommendations by the Governors' Committee. There could also be provision, as there is in other IMF matters, for action between Annual Meetings where urgency or orderliness so require.

The Governors' Committee would become the crucial center of this procedure. Again, as in the case of contributors, detailed rules for proportional representation would have to evolve from the lengthy negotiations of national representatives. No formula will be attempted here. But I would suggest two important elements. First, the Governors' Committee should include representation of the noncontributing countries, elected by a vote of all such countries, with a weight in the Committee voting of perhaps one-third. Second, all of the contributing countries should be individually represented, with their votes bearing some relationship to the cumulative total of their contributions (or initially, to their indicated original proportion among the contributors). As a practical matter, much of the work for which the Governors might take responsibility could be carried out by the respective IMF Executive Directors representing them; but I would not think that membership on the IMF Executive Board should be a prerequisite for inclusion among the countries actually serving on the Governors' Committee.

Resolving the issues on the locus of responsibility is a crucial prerequisite to consideration of the criteria that may then be relevant for determining the increments to be made to reserve assets from time to time. The reason is that no detachable separate formulas can do the job; the result will have to evolve out of the careful exercise of judgment by well-chosen men representing the full range of national experience that should be heard.

As I have already indicated in Chapter II, the process will require a judgment of over-all liquidity requirements, or at least of the changes in the amount of reserves needed at particular times, and of the extent to which reliance can or should be placed upon credit facilities in various circumstances. Countries will differ widely; each appraisal will require months of negotiation. Meanwhile, a number of other factors will be at work, affecting the volume of reserves and the areas of credit. I also suggested in Chapter II that any actual determination would have to be conditioned by what was in fact happening concurrently to the other factors affecting the volume of reserves, or the use of credit facilities. I urged that study of the measurements required should begin promptly within any of the international financial institutions or bodies now involved in various aspects of the liquidity question. And there is much to be learned, too, in these same bodies through attempting to measure now the needs for liquidity that might be provided through facilities already available.

Beyond stressing these essentials and the existing opportunities for gaining useful experience, I have no answers to propose for determining when, and by how much, changes in reserve assets should be made. I am quite certain, however, that the criteria which evolve from experience will be as different from, and as similar to, the original formulations as would emerge from a comparison between the formulation of Federal Reserve policy over the years, for example, and the criteria originally proposed a half-century ago. The shape of that record will have been very largely determined by the men who served, and in turn by the procedures through which their decision-making had to pass en route to the final conclusions.

Neither the approach I have suggested here for a money-creating facility that would preserve all of the elements of national sovereignty nor any other approach can be foolproof against the human capability for error or the propensity for excess. No simple rules relating the quantity of money to growing trade can, moreover, be a substitute for judgment, in international just as in domestic monetary management. But reliance upon this kind of review procedure within the framework of IMF responsibility and experience would at least ensure that the world would be able to create additional reserves, in a deliberate manner and in response to a full international debate concerning the magnitude of any current incremental need, whenever there was widespread agreement that existing reserves and available credit facilities did not provide adequate liquidity for the world economy.

Creating a New Secondary Reserve Asset

While the debate continues over the possibilities already outlined for creating another primary reserve asset which, alongside the dollar, might be "as good as gold," another fruitful area for exploration should also be kept in view. That is the possibility of creating a new secondary reserve asset, which could serve a useful purpose in the international monetary system. In several respects, solutions to some of the problems which it raises could become stepping stones to creating a secure new form of primary reserve asset. For the secondary reserve instrument has been suggested for a much narrower range of conditions: meeting a reserve shortage in a developed country; drawing funds only as volunteered by a few other developed countries; involving no sharing of decisions with less developed countries; not requiring, though potentially benefitting from, an association with the IMF; and not implying a commitment of indefinite duration.

What would this kind of secondary reserve asset be? There are three possible approaches: (1) special nonmarketable medium-term bonds; (2) consolidation loans; and (3) a long-term loan of reserve funds for monetary purposes.

1. *Special bonds—nonmarketable but redeemable.*

The first approach could be through the issuance of nonmarketable bonds by a reserve country in external deficit to the monetary authorities of countries whose currencies are basically strong and convertible. This the United States has done for several years, issuing some bonds to countries whose own reserves had just been increased by the proceeds of IMF drawings or, more importantly, to countries whose earned holdings of dollar reserves were very large or growing rapidly. In the latter case, bonds were often denominated in the currency of the investing country, thereby giving a formal exchange guaranty for the affected amounts. As a rule, maturities have thus far reached out only about two years, but could be longer with the agreement of both parties.

The operative clause in these bonds has been a provision permitting the holder, at his option, to convert the bonds into 90-day Treasury bills, and in turn to convert these particular bills on demand into cash on two days' notice. While the payment of interest on the bonds at rates in line with the corresponding U.S. maturities in the market has carried an implication that the bonds would indeed be held for the full term, the exigencies of central bank accounting have required these explicit provisions to assure that the bonds could qualify as appropriately liquid for central bank holding.

The bonds were issued in nonmarketable form in order to assure their use only for clearly verifiable holding by monetary authorities. To have permitted general transfer of these bonds, with their attractive terms, to holders among the general public abroad would have risked creating a conduit for drawing more dollars out of the United States. Commercial banks abroad could have made strong bids for the funds of American depositors, for example, in order to obtain more dollar funds to use in acquiring these special obligations. There would have been no net gain, only a drain, for the United States in such a circular flow. Moreover, the United States had to consider carefully its commitments in any given foreign currency, and preferred to have these limited to the official monetary authorities responsible for that currency. For example, it would not wish to be obligated in Italian lire, say, to investors who had acquired bonds for holding in Switzerland. If the United States government is to be obligated to Swiss holders, it can manage its own currency responsibilities most satisfactorily if the holder is the Swiss monetary authority, and the obligation is denominated in Swiss francs.

The concept underlying the use of these bonds as secondary reserves has had three important parts. One has been that the United States could, because of its unquestioned credit standing, borrow in this way to meet a part of its current deficit without calling upon the limited resources of the IMF. Orderly borrowing, while carrying the customary impetus for the debtor to correct its deficit and make repayment, also has enabled the creditor countries to acquire assets which they could consider an added part of their secondary reserves. These have become a second line of strength for use whenever the creditor's position might turn to deficit, as inevitably occurs in the irregular phasing of cyclical or secular changes among countries, even the leading industrialized ones.

A second part of the concept underlying the use of these bonds has been that a particular creditor country might, even before the United States had reached the position of being able to repay, find itself running into deficit. The bonds, while nonmarketable, are in effect shiftable, to the extent that the United States can seek out the country currently receiving some of the reserve gains, place its bonds with that country, and use the proceeds to retire the holdings of a country whose payments position may have deteriorated. That in fact happened during the spring of 1964 when bonds initially denominated in Italian lire were retired, during a period of balance-of-payments strain when Italy needed additional liquid reserves, with the proceeds of a corresponding new issue of bonds to the German Bundes-bank, denominated in German marks.

A third aspect has been that the use of these bonds began to inject the dollar, a reserve currency, into the active undertaking of obligations in other leading currencies. At a time when the United States was in deficit, and thus unable to acquire significant holdings of other convertible currencies as a means of multilateralizing participation in the process of reserve creation, the issuance of these bonds denominated in foreign currencies made a modest beginning toward the development of interlacing relationships between these other currencies and the international currency responsibilities of the United States. The continuance of large U.S. deficits in 1964, however, cast a shadow over the further use that might at that time have been made of this instrument as a useful element among others in providing a form of self-absorbing liquidity to finance swings between the United States and some of the other leading countries. But these bonds have at least served thus far as a useful and instructive probe into the territory of secondary reserve assets.

2. A consolidation loan.

This type of transaction has been proposed for two apparently contradictory but in fact complementary purposes: one, to fund an overhang of short-term liabilities, and the other, to convert an excess of reserves into a comfortable holding of reserve assets. To be quite explicit, a consolidation or funding of dollar liabilities has been proposed as a means of reducing some of the pressure of the continuing U.S. deficit. If several billions of volatile short-term dollar claims could be converted into a large long-term loan, it has been argued, the United States would have financed its regrettable but perhaps unavoidable deficits through straightforward borrowing. Primary reserve dollars would have been kept sufficiently scarce to eliminate the risks of speculative attacks upon the dollar. The world would settle back into the orderly use of short-term dollars for reserve purposes. And an underpinning of high quality assets of a longer-term nature would have been fitted into the portfolios of central banks or governments in a number of countries. In time of need on the part of other countries, these bonds could be marketed, or perhaps, if the U.S. balance were then strong, they might be called for repayment.

Some of the critics who have felt that the international monetary system was being undermined by a plethora of dollars, including many of the academic critics, have looked upon funding of this kind as a prerequisite to any meaningful reform of the system. Others have looked upon it as a way to keep the "dollar system" going, since they saw no reasonable possibility of any alternative. But the least publicized approach was probably the most meaningful—that a reserve currency, particularly during the early years of the return to convertibility, inevitably had to send out flying buttresses for support into the territory of the other leading currencies. The strains on a reserve currency were too varied and too unpredictable to be carried alone. The best temporizing approach, while awaiting further clarification of the design in which the world economy would develop, was to obtain this support by placing with some of these other countries a long-term loan and absorbing some of their perhaps glutted holdings of dollars (glutted, at least in comparison with the shortage still prevailing in much of the world).

Any funding of short-term dollar liabilities would presume, of course, deliberate and continuing action by the United States to reduce its deficit and balance its accounts. But if that could be assured, the issue would then become: would it be possible to invent a long-term instrument that could be held by central banks which traditionally can only hold short-term assets? One answer might be to attempt instead to persuade central banks to hold a second category of assets—assets that could be shiftable, or used as ready collateral for borrowing, without being short-dated. In their interim report of August 1964 the Deputies of the Group of Ten left the way open for further work to develop those possibilities. But they couched their interest more in terms of the third type of secondary reserve transaction.[5]

3. A long-term loan for monetary reserve purposes.

It was only a short step from the consolidation approach to the proposal of a long-term loan for the purpose of enlarging promptly the monetary reserves of a country that had outgrown the scale of its present reserves. The analogy was close—for such countries as the United Kingdom, or possibly Japan—to the position of a business concern that had invested so much, at home or abroad, that it needed a long-term loan for working capital purposes. The alternatives would be either a long and slow process of gradual reserve accumulation, with little margin for absorbing unexpected outlays and consequently little scope for the occasional venturesome risk, or a restrictionist policy designed to raise reserves more rapidly at the expense both of freely expanding world trade and of balanced domestic economic growth.

Problems of this nature are likely to persist within the international monetary system, whatever is decided as to the adequacy of reserves in general or even as to the adequacy of the usual types of short- and medium-term credit facilities. It might be impossible, without flooding many other countries in a sea of liquidity, to generate sufficiently large increases in total reserves to meet the legitimate needs of particular industrialized countries going through the much longer periods of structural adjustment that may become inevitable as industrial society becomes more complex.

For the less developed countries, there is at least an established framework of development aid and promotive foreign investment. As used, the recipients may feel that much is still wanting; but the framework does exist. For the new environmental problems of the highly developed economy, whose structural problems of readjustment may take long periods of time if the corrective changes are to be made without impairing the

[5] See Appendix, paragraphs 47 and 48.

spread of freedom in trade and payments relations, there may
well be need for something new. At any rate, the possibility is
sufficiently real to warrant the preparation of procedural arrangements capable of meeting such needs, if and when a group
of more developed countries should decide that a given country
should receive a long-term loan for enlarging its monetary reserves.

Assuming that the question of judgment concerning the capacity of the receiving country to make effective use of the loan
will, in any event, be exercised at the time by the creditor
countries, and that no formulation of criteria for that judgment
need be attempted here, there are two other important questions of principle on which thinking can usefully proceed at
an earlier stage. One relates to the medium of exchange which
the creditor countries will initially pay to the borrowing country,
and the terms which a borrowing country might undertake for
assuring a continuity of value until the time of ultimate repayment. The second concerns the uses which the creditor countries
might make of the loan instrument itself, as a part of their own
secondary reserves, while the long-term loan remains outstanding.

The original advance of additional reserve funds to a borrowing country could always, of course, be made in gold or in
dollars that the creditor countries might hold or acquire for the
purpose. If a new primary reserve asset were to be created,
such as a Fund Unit, that too could presumably be the medium
employed. The only real question concerns the appropriateness
of the suggestion sometimes heard that such a transfer be made
in the currencies of the creditor countries themselves. If such
an approach were followed, the loan might take the form of a
number of individual tranches, each denominated in a separate
currency, with other conditions of maturity and interest established on a uniform basis.

The purpose of such an arrangement would probably be to
enable the borrowing country explicitly to undertake repayment
to each creditor country in terms that would eventually provide

a value comparable to that maintained by each country for its own currency over the full life of the outstanding loan. The proponents of such an approach have at times gone even further, suggesting a multiple currency arrangement comparable to that used in a few recent bond issues in the private market in Europe. But it seems to me that the theoretical advantages of any such arrangements soon become lost in a tangle of technical complexities as the lawyers attempt to define all of the relevant terms for a variety of currencies—unless a form is developed comparable to that already suggested for the Fund Unit. Moreover, for its own operating purposes, the borrowing country would in all likelihood convert the proceeds into one or two widely accepted reserve assets so that it would receive no direct advantage itself from initially receiving a multiplicity of currencies. The ultimate obligation to repay should consequently, from the borrower's point of view, best be denominated in terms of those reserves which it intends to hold. For this purpose the gold-dollar at $35 per ounce would seem to represent the most satisfactory criterion both for the borrower and the lender.

If the borrower is prepared to give the lender a maintenance of value guaranty in terms of the original gold-dollars over the life of the loan, then it should be possible to find a way of endowing the loan instrument with qualities that could make it an appropriate asset for central bank holding. The need that any individual central bank would then face as a creditor, apart from satisfying the legal niceties of its own local legislation, would be to have assurance that in case its own reserve position were to weaken it could make use of its holding of this loan, in whole or in part, to meet the outpayments flowing from its own reserves. Central banks instinctively turn for such needs toward the possibility of arranging a rediscount facility or, failing that, to the assurance that a continuous market would be available for such an asset.

Insofar as the availability of rediscounting facilities for a long-term loan of this kind is concerned, one possibility would be for the borrowing country itself to undertake on demand to lend reserve funds, assuming that it was not in a position to make a partial repayment when called upon. As a second possibility, the suggestion has been made that the IMF should, in effect, provide a rediscount facility by permitting virtually automatic drawings against the collateral represented by such a loan. The difficulty with that approach, however, is that it would place a further potential burden or contingent claim upon the loanable funds available in the IMF without any corresponding increase in the supply of those funds. Member countries not included among the lenders participating in the long-term loan might reasonably contest the granting of preferred access to funds which they believe should be made available for the normal range of the IMF's customary lending activities.

A third possibility, apart from action to be taken by the borrower or by the IMF, would be for action among the group of lending countries themselves. This could take the form either of a rediscounting or of an actual sale. These would seem to offer the most promising lines for technical exploration. The arrangement might simply be that all the original members of the group participating in the loan would agree to "take each other out" in the event that the balance-of-payments position of any of the creditors required the use of those reserves which had originally been loaned on a long-term basis. The sticking point so far as actual purchase is concerned comes in providing adequate assurance that such transferability would be automatically available on the initiative of the creditor country in the light of its own judgment of need.

There should, of course, be a reasonable presumption that some of the original lenders would be enjoying ample reserve positions at such a time, so long as the original lending group included most of the leading industrial countries, since it is virtually a mathematical impossibility for all of them to be losing reserves and suffering balance-of-payments deterioration at the same time. Despite that likelihood, if the experience already observed in the formation of the Group of Ten can be taken as a lead (and there will be further evidence available on this score during 1965 when a decision must be reached on renewal of the General Arrangements to Borrow), no country is yet prepared to assume an obligation to purchase an unspecified amount of another asset at an unspecified time in the future.

It seems to me much more likely, however, that leading countries would be prepared to accept an obligation to lend against collateral of the kind involved here, on a short-term basis subject to renewal. If progress could be made toward acceptance of this kind of rediscounting obligation, on the basis that each member of the lending group would lend when called upon unless its own balance-of-payments position were critically weak and its reserves dwindling, the instrument arising from a long-term loan might qualify as an acceptable central banking asset. On these terms, there might then be meaningful possibilities for the transfer of substantial funds from the leading creditor countries into the monetary reserves of another industrialized country. In this sense the international monetary system might be able to generate an acceptable secondary reserve asset, to be acquired initially only by those countries with abundant reserves in periods of their own comparative external strength. A potentially distorting imbalance in the distribution of existing reserves might be partially redressed in that way, thereby providing a general stimulus to the increased flow of trade and payments not only among all of the industrialized countries but throughout the world.

As mentioned earlier, the most conspicuous possible candidates for long-term loans to increase their monetary reserves might be the United Kingdom and possibly Japan; there have also been suggestions at times that Canada might be interested in such arrangements. The overriding questions in any such specific case, once there is general agreement on the principles for creating such an asset, will be the questions of determining whether or not the particular borrowing country can be relied upon to make effective use of the proceeds, to fulfill the maintenance of value obligations, and to make repayment at maturity. There is, it seems to me, a reasonable basis for expecting valid needs for such long-term borrowing of reserves to emerge over the years ahead. Resolution of the issues of mechanics and principle in financial arrangements of this kind should be a valuable undertaking for the leading industrialized countries.

Harmonizing the Old and the New

The theme of these chapters has been that a need exists for orderly change. There is no desperate crisis upon us. Existing arrangements, as these have been elaborated over recent years, are serving well. But new kinds of needs are visible on the horizon. It is important that action move forward now to prepare to meet those needs when they arrive.

That is why it is not enough to be content with the already comprehensive and versatile facilities for creating additional reserves or providing additional credit among nations for monetary reserve purposes. That is why there should be, on the drawing boards of the IMF and of the monetary authorities of various countries, workable designs for new ways of creating primary reserves and for developing secondary reserves. But it should also be clear that designs of either kind are most difficult to work out, and that the areas for extended negotiation among nations are wide and varied. That is why, before I turn to a summing up in terms of the prospects for possible future steps along any of the lines I have discussed, I want to emphasize once more the many significant ways in which existing facilities can be more fully utilized, and some of them more widely elaborated, in order to assure the continued adequacy of international liquidity while the working out of other new plans goes forward. My concluding remarks will, consequently, be divided between those which identify important possibilities for the continual expansion of liquidity without taking additional action through further international compacts, and those possibilities emphasized in this chapter for introducing a new primary reserve asset or a new secondary reserve asset by means of new arrangements.

1. *The further potentials of present arrangements.*

In looking ahead toward the possibility of organized new facilities for bringing other countries into the center of the reserve currency system, I have deliberately underemphasized the important potentials that still remain for the growth of liquidity in a system dependent primarily upon the dollar for additional reserve assets, and upon the IMF primarily for credit facilities. I have, to be sure, stressed that the recent wariness of some countries concerning their dollar holdings would undoubtedly disappear with the achievement, for some months or years, of balance in the United States external accounts. I have also implied that there would be scope then for some cautious increases in the supply of United States dollars, as a means of consciously providing additional reserves, within a framework of group consultation broadly identified as "multilateral surveillance." I have not adequately stressed, however, the potentials for further growth in the use of dollars as reserve assets even if the United States itself remained in balance-of-payments equilibrium or surplus.

Those possibilities depend, of course, upon the readiness of the United States itself to acquire the obligations of other countries—to hold their currencies in its own monetary reserves, while at the same time paying out a corresponding amount of dollars for the general use of the world at large in meeting reserve needs. For the United States to undertake holdings of these other currencies on any substantial and growing scale would require the extension to these holdings of conditions comparable to whatever may have been bilaterally arranged by the United States in establishing its "swap lines" with each of the leading industrial countries. Of course, if another country were prepared to buy and sell gold freely at par to other monetary authorities and if it were an important trading area, the United States could hold that currency with a readiness comparable to that with which so many countries have for so long held dollars. But short of such initiatives by other countries, the United States would clearly have to require other forms of reasonable protection against the risks of change in the parity of any given currency, in return for the readiness of the United States to use that currency alongside gold in its own reserves. Such currencies would, in effect, be supporting the outstanding dollars that are in active service as official reserves—dollars that could also be readily usable in any foreign-exchange market by official or private accounts at any time, or convertible by monetary authorities into gold in the United States.

There has been occasion earlier to mention that the net effect of this method of providing additional dollar reserves would be neutral, so far as the U.S. balance-of-payments position is concerned. It would also be neutral with respect to the net indebtedness (or cash deficit) of the U.S. government, since each increase in liabilities would be matched by an increase in assets which the Treasury would presumably monetize through the Federal Reserve, retiring a corresponding amount of the Federal Reserve's holdings of U.S. government debt in the process. If monetized, the new currency acquisitions would also not result in any increase in the total outstanding debt subject to the statutory debt limit in this country. In order that there should be no net burden upon the budget of the United States, provision would have to be made in each bilateral negotiation for the payment of interest to the United States, on the holdings of foreign currency obligations which it had monetized, that would be at least equal to the interest paid on the U.S. Treasury debt issued to the foreign holders.

While there is no *prima facie* limit to the volume of dollars that the United States could issue for the use of the world in this way, the amounts would clearly have to be under close scrutiny, not merely in international bodies but more importantly here at home, to appraise the appropriate extent of the U.S. involvement in commitments of this kind. Proceeding cautiously, the experiment might reach the total of somewhat more than $1 billion already reached by the special bonds denominated in foreign currencies, and possibly become considerably larger. While the growth of credit facilities over the next several years will probably be proportionately more substantial than in the recent past, thereby reducing the size of needed increases in primary reserves, it is important to realize that further increases in dollars for reserve uses can occur on a considerable scale for some time, even though the United States persists in maintaining its external accounts in balance. Moreover, as I shall spell out in detail below, there is good reason to expect that a wholly practicable further extension of the IMF may well reduce the scale of any necessary dependence upon added dollars as the main source of primary reserves for some time to come.

The beginning has been satisfactorily made for each of the steps that would be needed to rely upon expanded holdings of foreign currencies by the United States for some part of the assurance of added world liquidity, in the form of primary reserves, over the years immediately ahead. There is, moreover, a very close analogy between this approach to an expanded supply of reserve assets and the technique already suggested for the introduction of a new Fund Unit. Under this approach, just as under that suggested for a Fund Unit, a usable reserve asset would be created in amounts corresponding to holdings of other currencies that would be pooled to support the issuance of the new reserves. The principal differences would be those arising from the fact that no new international agreements would be necessary and no reserve asset of a new and unfamiliar character would have to be introduced.

While presumably any addition to reserves through this approach would be subjected to the screening of multilateral surveillance, the selection of particular currencies would depend upon a succession of bilateral understandings between the United States and each of the other countries whose currencies are involved. There would be no set or continuing formulation determining the amount of any other currency taken into the pool of holdings being assembled by the United States. There would be no problem of transferability between this reserve asset and a vehicle currency, since the dollar is actively in use for both kinds of purposes.

The drawbacks would be those primarily of control and organization. The Fund Unit, if arrangements could be worked out along lines already indicated, would be the result of carefully considered international agreements; each increment would be carefully appraised by the broadest possible group of affected countries; and the risk of undue dependence upon, or undue influence exerted by, the United States would be avoided. Nonetheless, as a way station on the route toward establishment of a Fund Unit, the creation of dollars against holdings of other currencies by the United States would offer an opportunity for experimentally moving forward on several of the important elements of the Fund Unit technique, while the broader questions might still be undergoing lengthy negotiation prior to the culmination of satisfactory procedures for the introduction of the Fund Unit itself.

Paralleling this important avenue for further use of already existing arrangements, there is the great potential of the IMF itself for creating primary reserves—a potential that has, quite unaccountably, been consistently passed over by critics who seem to insist upon dramatic new developments in their search for ways to improve the international monetary system. They recognize the important and useful role of the IMF's credit facilities; they endorse continuing increases in the IMF's quotas in order to assure periodic enlargement of its capacity for extending credit; but they ignore the other side of that credit extension. Whenever the IMF makes use of the currency of a member country by paying that currency out to another member that is making a drawing, the country whose currency has been used automatically acquires a corresponding improvement in its reserve position. And in many cases, though not all, the over-all effect is an addition to the global total of reserve assets.[6]

If the country whose currency is drawn should already be in debt to the IMF, then the drawing of its currency amounts to

[6] For a summary description of the purposes, principles and procedures of the IMF see Appendix, paragraphs 16 and 17.

an automatic repayment of its debt by that amount. But if the country whose currency is used has not been in debt to the IMF, then it acquires additional drawing rights corresponding to the full amount of its currency used. These are colloquially referred to as "super gold tranche" drawing rights, and the country whose currency has been used by the IMF is free to use its "super gold tranche" virtually on demand. Under a clarification of gold tranche procedures that the Executive Board issued in 1964, this means in technical terms that whenever the IMF's holdings of a given currency drop below 75 per cent of its quota, the country responsible for that currency acquires a drawing right that has all the requisites of an immediately usable reserve asset. So long as there is a growing use of the IMF by drawing countries, therefore, some contributing countries can receive growing additions to their own reserves in super gold tranche drawing rights. This was in earlier years an important source of reserves for the United States—reserves which were used in turn to finance a part of our own deficits from 1958 until 1962.

The other 25 per cent of any country's quota represents, of course, its own "gold tranche." This is the amount of its quota that a country is expected to pay for originally in gold, or more broadly, to pay out of its own reserves. Thus, properly speaking, the ordinary gold tranche does not itself constitute an additional reserve. It has been, to the extent that it represents a usable gold tranche claim, already paid for by the member country out of its own reserves. Moreover, although the IMF may later pay out the gold which it originally received, the gold tranche claim remains as an additional reserve asset. The regular gold tranche is also virtually available on demand, just as the "super gold tranche" is. The difference is that a drawing under the regular gold tranche carries an obligation to repay; the super gold tranche does not.

There are, however, additional ways in which the regular gold tranche claims of a member might be increased, without making an actual related payment from the member's own reserves. The

IMF could decide, by action of its Executive Board, to extend the same virtually automatic drawing rights that a country now has "within its gold tranche," to some part of what are called its "credit tranches." These latter are the counterpart of the payment that each country has made to the IMF in its own currency. That is, as already noted, a country acquires regular "gold tranche" drawing rights for the 25 per cent of quota paid out of its own reserves; but paralleling the other 75 per cent, which it pays into the IMF in its own currency, it acquires "credit tranches," with each "tranche" viewed as a 25 per cent slice of the total quota. As a rule, a country can readily draw on the IMF for its first credit tranche, but the scrutiny and conditions become more demanding as a country requests drawings that use more and more of its credit tranches. Drawings may in practice, on the paying in of still more of the drawing country's currency, extend on through to a fourth credit tranche, and in special cases may exceed that amount.

Clearly, one way that the IMF could enlarge primary reserves would be to give to some part of the first credit tranche the same status of drawing rights that now applies only to the "gold tranche." That is, instead of limiting a country to those virtually automatic drawing rights which it acquires by the paying in of its own reserves (i.e., the regular gold tranche) and to the claims arising because the IMF has paid out some of its own currency (the "super gold tranche") the IMF could declare, for example, that an additional 5 per cent of total quota was available on gold tranche terms. As a parallel action, the upper limit of available credit tranches might also be raised.

There is still another method for virtually creating primary reserves which the IMF might consider, although probably the counsel of prudence would suggest an amendment of the Articles of Agreement if this were to be attempted. This other possibility would occur at the time that a general increase was being made in the quotas of all members. In such circumstances, the IMF might permit a member to pay for the gold tranche portion (i.e., one quarter of its subscription) with a gold certificate, or perhaps to use such a certificate for some portion of the gold tranche payment. Under the terms of the certificate the member would undertake to pay gold on demand to the IMF and could agree to maintain gold holdings of at least a corresponding amount in its own reserves. But it would not actually pay gold out of its own reserves as part of the quota subscription, for any part covered by the certificate. Under ordinary conditions the country would not have to expect to be called upon for payment of the gold. Provision might, moreover, be made that such calls, if they were to be invoked, would on any particular call be only for part, not all, of the amounts pledged.

Thus possibilities exist within the structure of the IMF's present credit facilities, for introducing new methods of creating additional primary reserve assets. Whether or not the IMF were to grant gold tranche drawing rights to some part of the existing credit tranches, and whether or not the gold certificate device might be used, the normal workings of the IMF lead to the creation of primary reserves in the purely routine manner that I have described. This is, moreover, a creation of primary reserves that arises only out of credits that have been granted for monetary purposes under conditions that meet IMF standards of monetary accountability. There is an appealing logic in depending, as fully as possible, upon this means for the conscious creation of additional liquidity.

Indeed, with this range of possibilities available within the present structure of the IMF, one might reasonably question the need for introducing all of the additional apparatus implied by the introduction of a new Fund Unit—the establishment within the IMF of what I have earlier compared to the issue department of some central banks. Clearly, to whatever extent the IMF can be more intensively used along existing lines, there is at least an additional gaining of time for working out the many questions of principle and of operating procedure that must necessarily be resolved before a Fund Unit could be practicably created. Moreover, as additional experience is gained with the further use of presently existing IMF potentials, that experience will assuredly strengthen the design of any new arrangements that might ultimately be introduced.

There are several reasons for believing, however, that an eventual turn toward reliance upon a Fund Unit will be desirable, even though increasing use may also be made of all the IMF's existing potentialities. Indeed, the dependence of contributing shares to the Fund Unit in part upon the uses made of various currencies in IMF drawings, itself establishes a close operating interdependence. Perhaps the most significant reason for turning to a Fund Unit, in terms of the criticisms most widely expressed concerning the present reserve currency system, is that the introduction of a Fund Unit would permit an explicit international determination of an important quantitative element in over-all monetary reserves from time to time. Thus, what have been called the unplanned or unguided elements in reserve creation, described at some length in the first chapter, could be in large measure overcome. To be sure, all of the presently existing factors affecting the creation of reserves could continue to operate. To the extent that these are in fact unguided, that characteristic would presumably continue. But with the introduction of the Fund Unit there would always be an opportunity for a duly constituted international body to make some additional changes at the margin, in order either to supplement what had been more or less accidentally produced in one period, or possibly to offset an excessive creation of reserves that had occurred through the unguided workings of the rest of the mechanism in another period. The opportunity and the arrangements would be available whenever agreement could be reached among the nations of the world on the further amount of primary reserves that should be created.

No doubt, when actually able to make such changes, the monetary authorities of the world would find that there is no generally acceptable criterion or set of criteria for determining what the changes ought to be. They would probably discover that the same aggregate amount of reserves can have different significance at different times, depending upon the intensity (or veloc-

III/AN AGENDA FOR THE FUTURE

119

ity) with which existing reserves are employed. Nonetheless, the existence of Fund Unit facilities would assure the world that there need never be a time when, through lack of adequate operational arrangements, it had to stand by powerless to act when a widespread consensus existed that a change of some roughly agreed magnitude was needed in the aggregate supply of monetary reserves available to support the world's work.

Another related advantage of developing the Fund Unit, alongside everything else that is now available under existing monetary arrangements, is that it would provide, at least for this marginal element of additional reserve assets, an opportunity for countries to share in the initial and continuing responsibility for reserve asset creation on terms that would assure a reasonably equitable distribution of shares among the contributing countries. At least if the suggestions made earlier in this chapter were to be followed, contributions would be related in some approximate way to the recent patterns of use already made of the various currencies eligible for a share in the contributions. Such an allocation would have much to recommend it for the actual creation of a reserve asset, as against the negotiated allocations among nations that determine the distribution of regular IMF quotas in the IMF.

If gold tranche claims in the IMF were to become the principal means of adding to primary reserve assets, there would be a risk, moreover, that every country would be given a strong incentive to attempt to negotiate a larger quota for itself at the time of each quinquennial review of the IMF quotas. Some countries would look upon the quota negotiation as an opportunity to exercise diplomatic skill or trading ability in order to get a larger—and in a sense "free"—holding of primary reserves, perhaps without regard to other appropriate criteria for determining the distribution of quotas among the members. While in practice the risks of that kind of laxity by agreement might not prove to be great, they would surely increase if this were the primary or sole means through which added fiduciary reserves could be obtained for meeting the growth requirements of the expanding world economy.

By contrast, under the Fund Unit approach, countries would earn their shares in the new Unit Account by having previously contributed their own currencies to international monetary uses through normal operations. Countries which had not already met the self-qualifying test of the marketplace by providing currencies that could be effectively used by other countries—that is, countries who had not in previous years been able or prepared to see flows of their own currencies for monetary purposes result in added claims upon their real resources by other countries—would not automatically obtain any of the new reserve asset. Instead, these countries would receive their shares of the newly created asset after its initial distribution by earning them through trade or by qualifying for them through meeting the credit standards or the aid requirements judged appropriate by the creditor countries themselves. In this way the essential reliance upon the principles of national sovereignty, and upon the principles of balance-of-payments discipline, would have been most effectively reinforced.

There would, to be sure, also be possibilities for distortion or abuse under the Fund Unit approach. Nothing has been, and presumably nothing will ever be, impeccable in the arrangements evolved by the world for meeting its monetary needs. However, it does seem to me that the path of evolutionary development might reasonably be expected to lead from the fuller use of everything now available in the international monetary system toward the introduction of a new reserve asset—an asset that could be built upon the added experience still to be obtained from further elaboration of all the facilities that are already at work.

2. *The implementation of reforms.*

The monetary authorities of the world have an unusual opportunity. Well in advance of any possible impairment of the functions of the monetary system, widespread attention has been focussed on the need for constructive change. A welcoming climate of opinion has developed. Official bodies have for some two years already been actively exploring the avenues for potential future progress. In these circumstances a new fusion of effort should be possible and productive.

Whether a further spur to world agreement occurs only within the IMF, or also in the Group of Ten, or in other bodies, is not crucial. What matters is that full liaison be assured among all intergovernmental negotiations, and that all press forward. There is ample time for deliberation, but not for procrastination. Governments must recognize that uncertainty over the future path of monetary evolution can itself, if it continues long, become a disruptive force. A new, declarative resolution of agreement is needed to set benchmarks for the next decade or two that will be as clear, and as impelling, as those originally set at Bretton Woods in 1944; not as inconclusive and ambiguous as those attempted at Genoa in 1922.

Once agreement is reached on the general nature of the need for any additional reserve asset, on the kind of reserve asset to be sought, and on those lasting principles of the existing system with which it should be made compatible, much will remain for the hard negotiations which must precede the instituting of workable detailed arrangements. But again, the monetary authorities of the world have an unusual opportunity. Once agreed on the broad outlines of their ultimate objective, they can select from several present possibilities the elements of an intermediate program that can assure adequate and flexible liquidity arrangements while the lengthier deliberations are in progress. And they can so design such a transitional program that experience gained in its implementation will help to resolve many of the issues confronting the negotiators at work on the longer-run design.

The innovation and experimentation of the past four or five years, centering so largely on the dollar or originating so largely in concern over the continued United States deficits, have helped to set the stage for both the transitional and the more fundamental changes. But it is a new and different stage, and must remain so—a stage that will no longer be covered over with dollars that have resulted from overlong and overlarge United States deficits; a stage on which other currencies must play a larger role and assume more burdensome responsibilities, consistent with the new strength of the economies of their own countries.

The transitional arrangements can make use of many of the recent innovations; a number will in fact be in service, meeting the full scale of impending reserve needs for some time to come, whether or not any specific further action is taken. And the enlargement of IMF quotas that is in process during 1965 will add a useful larger dimension to the credit facilities that serve so many and to the reserve assets which are created as the IMF pays out strong and usable currencies. In addition, there is the scope already outlined for the possible further issuance of dollars against an acquisition by the United States of a bouquet of various foreign currencies.

There is also another kind of change that could usefully be introduced by the IMF, although it would no doubt require an amendment of the IMF's Articles of Agreement, and would consequently fall within the category of "reforms" rather than that of adaptations in present procedures. This change would call upon the IMF to establish facilities for receiving deposits from the monetary authorities of countries in strong reserve and balance-of-payments positions. Such a deposit by any given country could appropriately be made only in its own currency. The deposit of the currency of another country would, indeed, conflict with the essential sovereignty principles which have been stressed and respected throughout the suggestions made in this book.

Through the deposit of its own currency, however, a country could conceivably both provide the IMF with additional resources for meeting the growing credit needs of expanding world trade and, at the same time, acquire for itself an asset roughly equivalent to its super gold tranche position. Such an approach, while much looser than the arrangements suggested for establishing a Fund Unit Account, would nevertheless be very close to it in principle. In each approach there would be a voluntary agreement to place one's own currency on deposit with the IMF. Presumably, each would, or could, embody a maintenance of gold value obligation to the IMF. And if another intermediate technique should seem needed, or if disagreement over the elements of a Fund Unit concept should become prolonged, a turn toward the use of voluntary deposits would seem quite promising.

There would be significant differences, of course. Each deposit arrangement could be bilaterally agreed upon between the IMF and the particular country. The amounts might or might not approximate any generally agreed guide as to the total increment in reserve assets to be desired, nor could there be any assurance that deposits once made would remain in being as a lasting source of added liquidity. The deposit claim itself, unlike the Fund Unit, would not be transferable, although the depositing country could use its other reserves more freely while holding the IMF claim and could draw other currencies from the IMF in turn. The IMF for its part would have a larger supply of strong currencies to use in meeting any kind of drawing requests from other countries. But it might find itself vulnerable to large drawings made at the initiative of depositing countries.

There might be some danger, too, that countries would be so attracted by the prospect of gaining in this way all of the benefits of a quota increase, without necessarily making any contribution out of their own reserves, that periodic and uniform over-all IMF quota increases for all countries would become more difficult to achieve. In general, the advantages would seem to fall heavily on the side of the contributing country, with less prospect of working out the kinds of *quid pro quo* conditions which the Fund Unit approach could require in order to help buttress other elements of the system. Nonetheless, as a means of providing the IMF with some additional capacity to absorb or cushion the large shifts of capital from country to country that seem likely to characterize a convertible world, the deposit technique could be very useful. It could provide added flexibility and growth for the international monetary system, if the agenda outlined in the first two sections of this chapter proves too ambitious.

The balance of advantage seems to me to lie, however, in setting the world's sights on a comprehensive approach that risks no weakening of any of the structural elements of the system as we know it today, provides some opportunity for actual strengthening of that system, and then goes on to develop an assured framework for the deliberate creation of reserve assets on the basis of international action whenever there is sufficient agreement that a need for more reserves exists.

The Fund Unit approach, linked as it is to the commitments of individual countries and their continuing obligations (once originally assumed), provides safeguards against the risks of over-issue that are not to be found in most of the plans which propose, simply, that the IMF or some other international entity be empowered to create money which the nations of the world should bind themselves in perpetuity to accept. Nor does the Fund Unit approach, unlike many of the proposals that have been made, hinge the creation of new reserve assets directly to aid or investment in the less developed countries, with the attendant risk of being subjected to an understandable urge for over-issue.

There would be full assurance to anyone acquiring Fund Units that a pool of assets of the highest quality was permanently held against the full value of the outstanding amount of Fund Units. This, it seems to me, is the only safe way to approach the awesome possibility of creating an international money, which will depend for its acceptance on assured confidence on the part of all who use it.

It should be reasonable, while work goes forward on the creation of primary reserves, to look forward to parallel advantages in the development of arrangements for instituting a new secondary reserve asset, possibly along the lines of the long-term loan for monetary reserve purposes. If that could be done, the first opportunity for its use might possibly arise in connection with the drawings of the United Kingdom on the IMF that will have totalled some $2.4 billion by the middle of 1965. While it is conceivable that the United Kingdom could accomplish full repayment within the customary 3- to 5-year period, there might be a general consensus among the leading industrialized countries before that maturity is reached that both the progress of recovery in the British balance of payments and the orderliness of world trade conditions as a whole would be better served if Britain were able to repay over a longer period, and could meanwhile maintain larger reserves of its own.

Thus the first opportunity for granting a long-term loan for monetary reserve purposes might be one in which some or all of the countries whose currencies were used by the IMF to meet Britain's drawings of 1964 and 1965 were to join together to make a long-term loan to the United Kingdom. Such a loan, running for ten or fifteen or twenty years, in an amount equivalent to several billions of dollars, could enable Britain both to discharge its full remaining obligation to the IMF and also to increase its current operating balances.

All of this depends, of course, on satisfactory progress in resolving the other questions of principle concerning a loan of this kind that I have already discussed. Presumably the initiative for further work on these questions could, quite appropriately, come from the Group of Ten countries themselves, perhaps augmented by other countries whose currencies were used in the British drawings of 1964 and 1965.

Concluding Observations

In this survey of the possibilities for monetary reform in the modern world economy, I have committed many errors of omission. For one, I have not attempted to analyze specifically any of the well-known and widely publicized specific plans—those of Triffin or Stamp or Harrod or Bernstein or Maudling, for example, or many others including a proposal suggested in various forms by representatives of the French government and identified as a "collective reserve unit." I have freely plagiarized from the analysis underlying many of these and from the details embodied in some of them, without attempting at each step of the way to identify the genealogy of particular ideas as they have appeared in one or another of the various writings. I have also adapted, in ways that seem to me most likely to fulfill the conditions necessary for continuing monetary order, aspects of such general proposals as those for the issuance of IMF debentures, or the granting of special gold guaranties, or arrangements for a transferability of quotas or claims on the IMF.

The various suggestions made in this book are intended to meet the sovereignty requirements, the confidence requirements, and the essential and continuing operating requirements of the monetary system to which the world has become accustomed. I hope these suggestions also fall inside an area that is still open for meaningful negotiation among all countries, large or small, industrialized or developing.

In the course of this review it should also have been made abundantly clear that any effort toward international management of the creation of reserve assets will be much more intricate and much more sensitive than the effort upon which so much of the world has been engaged for so much of the past twenty years to restore convertibility and to manage the availability of international credit facilities through the IMF. The creation of money inevitably carries with it the risk of dissipation and excess, as well as the risk of inadequacy and constriction. The granting of credit carries with it, in an important degree, a kind of built-in protection that is not present when the hard decision must be made to create or not to create additional money by deliberate action. For credit must be repaid: the credit-worthiness of the borrower is at stake; the soundness of the lending institution remains under continual surveillance.

If there is to be a new mechanism for the creation of money which does not embody the disciplines of a parallel creation of credit, the design of that structure will demand the best efforts of the best-equipped financial representatives of all governments. It should, at the least, embody arrangements to assure the sustained linkage between that money and gold at a price equivalent to $35 per ounce. It would be presumptuous of any one person, writing alone, to attempt to draft a detailed plan, or even to draw a detailed sketch, for the full range of measures and arrangements that such a structure will require. It is essential, however, to focus attention on a number of the principles that such an effort will have to take into account, as well as on the issues which it will have to resolve.

Perhaps, if a way can be found toward agreement on conditions for the contributions of currencies and for the participation of various countries in the key decisions, a usable new reserve asset can eventually be fitted into place alongside gold, dollars, and any other currency that serves for reserve purposes, and be used interchangeably with them. It is also possible, if the contributing countries accept a commitment both to sell and to buy gold at their established parities and to accept as well as to pay out their holdings of any new units, that a gradual harmonization may develop among the gold reserve ratios of the contributing countries, thereby helping to advance further the long search for ways of economizing on the limited supply of gold that must serve as the center of gravity for a dramatically expanding international monetary system. No simple agreement on percentages, without the reinforcement of some other arrangements comparable to the suggestions here, would be likely to prove effective—except perhaps in drawing more gold from the U.S. reserves. And every one-percentage-point increase in the average ratios of gold to total reserves, for the other members of the IMF, would absorb about one-half billion dollars of gold.

It will be as important in the future as it was at the end of World War II that any country or countries which, for whatever reason, hold a disproportionate part of the total gold reserves of the world, should find practicable ways to assist a constructive redistribution. Otherwise, a growing concentration of gold, in holdings that are virtually withdrawn from use, will impose a distorting strain not only on the functioning of the international monetary system, but also upon that flourishing of trade and payments throughout the world which the system exists to serve.

Alongside this pattern of possible developments, there will undoubtedly be need, too, for occasional deliberate action to effect an equalizing of the distribution of reserves among some of the leading countries through long-term loans. And, hopefully, means can be found, in principle, for meeting that need in ways that will help to maintain the balanced development of the monetary system.

Even if great progress can be made along these or similar lines, we will have to be reconciled to the inescapable fact that the fulfillment of any such process must take time. Just as the IMF itself did not become fully and widely operational for nearly a decade after its origination, so we must also expect that new arrangements of this far-reaching import may need some years for exploratory initial use, even after the arrangements for installing them have been agreed upon. Once a body of some kind is charged with the responsibility for creating a new international money, the early deliberations will undoubtedly consume many months before even the first decision on a first installment can be reached.

Meanwhile, the world can take full satisfaction in the fact that the existing international monetary system is fully adequate to the range of tasks confronting it. The assignment for the future is to add upon, not to displace, the present constellation of relationships among national currencies, vehicle currencies, reserve currencies, and the International Monetary Fund. In this, there is great encouragement to be found in the momentum that has already been developed through the past few years of meaningful and deepening international cooperation.

Underlying all that may be done by the international monetary system, and any changes that may be made in this system, there will still be an ultimate dependence upon the performance of each individual economy and its own domestic monetary system. No rearrangement of international monetary facilities, and no heightening of international financial cooperation, can ever take the place of the responsibility which each individual country must bear for maintaining the viability of its own economy. There is no monetary escape route from the elements of economic discipline—neither within nor among countries. Any innovations in the international monetary system, if they are to be successful and sustainable, will have to reinforce the discipline of the marketplace within each individual country while they also reach out to enlarge, or to redistribute, the supply of international liquidity. This, it seems to me, is in the Elihu Root tradition—a tradition of evolutionary progress, dependent upon interaction between the sovereign responsibilities of nations and the expanding opportunities for international action.

In 1898, the year before Elihu Root first became a Cabinet officer in the United States, Knut Wicksell in Sweden wrote this telling conclusion to his book on *Interest and Prices:* ". . . the question of monetary reform on rational lines definitely remains among the most important of economic problems. That its realization depends on international cooperation, which would have to be both permanent and somewhat thorough in nature, is to my mind a positive recommendation . . . for it adds one more safeguard for the preservation and strengthening of . . . international peace." [7]

[7] Knut Wicksell, *Interest and Prices,* tr. by R. F. Kahn (London: Macmillan, 1936), p. 196; original title, *Geldzins und Güterpreise* (1898).

APPENDIX

Ministerial Statement
of the Group of Ten

and

Annex Prepared by Deputies

10th August 1964

M. Valéry GISCARD D'ESTAING, Ministre des Finances et des Affaires Economiques of France, acting as Chairman of the Ministers and Governors of the Group of Ten countries participating in the General Arrangements to Borrow, today issued the following Statement. There is included with this Statement an Annex prepared by Deputies of the Group of Ten.

Ministerial Statement

1. The Ministers and Governors of the ten countries participating in the General Arrangements to Borrow have, over the past year, examined, with a long-range perspective, the wider implications of the obligations which they have accepted for helping to assure the stability and adequacy of the international payments system. They have reviewed the functioning of the international monetary system and its probable future needs for liquidity. The necessary studies were entrusted to a Group of Deputies, to be carried out in cooperation with the International Monetary Fund and with the participation of representatives of the staffs of the International Monetary Fund, the Organization for Economic Cooperation and Development, and the Bank for International Settlements, as well as of an observer of the Swiss National Bank. The conclusions and decisions of the Ministers and Governors were greatly assisted by these studies, the results of which are described in the accompanying Annex.

2. In reviewing the functioning of the international monetary system, the Ministers and Governors reaffirmed their conviction that a structure based, as the present is, on fixed exchange rates and the established price of gold, has proved its value as a foundation on which to build for the future. They further agreed that increasingly close cooperation among monetary authorities was an essential element supporting the system. As concerns liquidity, the Ministers and Governors are agreed that, for the international monetary system as a whole, supplies of gold and reserve currencies are fully adequate for the present and are likely to be for the immediate future. These

reserves are supplemented by a broad range of credit facilities. The continuing growth of world trade and payments is likely to entail a need for larger international liquidity. This need may be met by an expansion of credit facilities and, in the longer run, may possibly call for some new form of reserve asset.

3. The smooth functioning of the international monetary system depends on the avoidance of major and persistent international imbalances and on the effective use of appropriate policies by national governments to correct them when they occur. The Ministers and Governors have therefore decided to initiate a thorough study of the measures and instruments best suited for achieving this purpose compatibly with the pursuit of essential internal objectives. In view of the experience it has already acquired in this field, Working Party 3 of the O.E.C.D. is being invited to take charge of this study.

4. A significant development in the evolution and strengthening of the system has been the emergence of a wide range of bilateral and multilateral credit facilities, notably to cope with speculative movements and sudden pressures. There has at the same time been increasing recognition of the fact that the way in which balance of payments deficits and surpluses are financed has implications for countries other than those directly concerned. The Ministers and Governors have consequently agreed on the usefulness of participating, through the international institutions which are already concerned with these problems, in a "multilateral surveillance" of the ways and means of financing balance of payments disequilibria. To this end, they have approved arrangements which will give the monetary authorities of countries participating in them a more comprehensive and up-to-date view of major trends and will afford them a better basis for strengthening their policy cooperation in the international monetary sphere. This should help them to avoid excesses or shortages in the means of financing surpluses or deficits in the balance of payments, as well as to discuss measures appropriate for each country in accordance with the general economic outlook. The Ministers and Governors of the Group will meet from time to time to survey current developments in this field.

5. Looking further into the future, since there is a possibility that the supply of gold and foreign exchange reserves may prove to be inadequate for the over-all reserve needs of the world econ-

omy, the Ministers and Governors, without prejudging any aspect of this question, have approved the arrangements made by their Deputies for a study group to examine various proposals regarding the creation of reserve assets either through the I.M.F. or otherwise.

6. Finally, the Ministers and Governors have exchanged views on the adequacy of international credit arrangements. The International Monetary Fund, with large resources of credit and a code of obligations, occupies a central position. In order to further the Fund's capabilities and while recognizing that the responsibility for decisions concerning the provision of additional resources rests with the competent authorities of the I.M.F., itself, the Ministers and Governors, for their part, are agreed that they will, in the forthcoming quinquennial review of Fund quotas during 1965, support a moderate general increase in member quotas. At the same time, they will support relative adjustments of those individual quotas which are clearly out of line. In addition, the Deputies are instructed to study the questions related to the renewal of the General Arrangements to Borrow and to make recommendations to the Ministers and Governors before September, 1965.

7. The Ministers and Governors believe that the review of the international monetary system conducted during the past year has helped to clarify the fundamental considerations which underlie the various national points of view and has brought a fuller recognition of common interests. They believe that the spirit and practice of cooperation that have now been achieved warrant confidence that fully adequate, but not excessive, resources will be made available to meet the liquidity requirements of the world as a whole. This readiness of their countries to work together in meeting unexpected developments or longer range requirements will strengthen the capacity of the international monetary system to support and sustain the objectives of growth, employment, and price stability that are shared among all people.

Annex Prepared by Deputies

This document presents the main results of the studies of the Deputies, which led to the report presented by them to the Ministers and Governors at their meeting in Paris on June 15-16, 1964.

Introduction

1. Our Group was established by Ministers and Governors, as recorded in their communiqué of 2nd October 1963, in the following terms:

In reviewing the longer-run prospects, the Ministers and Governors agreed that the underlying structure of the present monetary system—based on fixed exchange rates and the established price of gold—has proven its value as the foundation for present and future arrangements. It appeared to them, however, to be useful to undertake a thorough examination of the outlook for the functioning of the international monetary system and of its probable future needs for liquidity. This examination should be made with particular emphasis on the possible magnitude and nature of the future needs for reserves and for supplementary credit facilities which may arise within the framework of national economic policies effectively aiming at the objectives mentioned in paragraph 2. The studies should also appraise and evaluate various possibilities for covering such needs.

The objectives mentioned in paragraph 2 of the communiqué were as follows:

The Ministers and Governors reaffirmed the objective of reaching such balance at high levels of economic activity with a sustainable rate of economic growth and in a climate of price stability.

We have also regarded certain passages in the same communiqué as relevant to our studies:

The Ministers and Governors noted that the present national reserves of member countries, supplemented as they are by the resources of the IMF, as well as by a network of bilateral facilities, seemed fully adequate in present circumstances to cope with possible threats to the stability of the international payments system.
The Ministers reviewed the "General Arrangements to Borrow" in the International Monetary Fund and reiterated their determination that these resources would be available for decisive and prompt action.
The Ministers and Governors believe that such an examination of the international monetary system will further strengthen inter-

national financial cooperation, which is the essential basis for the continued successful functioning of the system.

Our instructions were that:

Any specific suggestions resulting from the studies by the Deputies will be submitted to the Ministers and Governors for consideration.

2. In accordance with these instructions a number of meetings were held during the past year and close relations were maintained with the International Monetary Fund (IMF), the Organization for Economic Cooperation and Development (OECD) and the Bank for International Settlements (BIS). The staffs of these institutions have been represented in our discussions and have made valuable contributions to the work of the Group. The discussions also benefited from the presence of representatives of the Swiss National Bank, as decided by Ministers following completion of the legislation looking to Swiss cooperation with the General Arrangements to Borrow.

3. A review was made of the major proposals put forward in recent years for reform of the existing international payments system, ranging from a restoration of the former gold standard to the setting up of an international central bank with supra-national authority. While no single plan appeared to meet the requirements in a way fully consistent with the general political, economic and social environment in which international payments and arrangements must operate, we have found much in the analysis underlying these various approaches that has been useful and stimulating for our discussions and appraisal.

4. Our report, after examining the broader economic and financial structure within which the international monetary system must operate, surveys briefly the major aspects of the system as it has evolved in the postwar world, makes an appraisal of the present system, explores lines of future development and, finally, sets forth and explains our major conclusions and recommendations.

I. The Importance of International Balance and the Process of Adjustment

5. The smooth functioning of the international monetary system depends on the avoidance of major and persistent imbalances and on the effective use of appropriate policies by national governments to

correct them when they occur. The process of adjustment and the need for international liquidity are closely interrelated. If there is not enough liquidity, countries may not have time to make adjustments in an orderly fashion, and may be forced into measures that are disruptive both to their domestic economies and to international economic relationships. If, on the other hand, there is too much liquidity, the adjustment mechanism may function too slowly, and a delay in taking measures necessary to restore balance will in the end be harmful at home as well as abroad. In view of this close interdependence, we have thought it right, before proceeding to examine the international monetary system itself, to look into the processes and procedures for maintaining balance of payments equilibrium, and for correcting imbalances when they occur.

6. The objectives of economic policy in a free society are broad and complex. They include healthy and sustainable economic growth, full and efficient employment, together with goals in the fields of social development, defense policy, and foreign aid. But continuing success in the pursuit of these objectives demands reasonable price stability and equilibrium in the over-all balance of international payments. Countries will nevertheless from time to time find themselves showing a tendency toward a sustained deficit or a sustained surplus on their over-all balance of payments, and in order to counteract this tendency they will find it necessary to make use of an appropriate combination of the following instruments of economic policy:

—Budgetary and fiscal policies;
—Incomes policies;
—Monetary policies;
—Other measures relating to international capital transactions (e.g., measures designed to affect capital movements, advance repayments of inter-governmental debts, etc.);
—Commercial policies (e.g., temporary unilateral tariff reductions and similar measures);
—Selective policies directed to particular sectors of the economy (e.g., housing or hire purchase, governmental transactions affecting the balance of payments, etc.).

7. Such instruments must be employed with proper regard for obligations in the field of international trade and for the IMF obligation to maintain stable exchange parities which are subject to

change only in cases of fundamental disequilibrium. A "mix" of policies appropriate to both internal and external objectives has to be found and applied by national governments. It falls to each government to ensure that it is fully equipped with the various policy instruments necessary to its task, to be alert to the dangers of delay in making use of these instruments, and to put appropriate weight on the maintenance of external equilibrium without neglecting internal objectives. It is thus for each government individually to find means of reconciling its own social priorities, institutional practices and general economic performance with the ever-present need for external equilibrium. It is for governments collectively to consider how the actions of each may affect others and whether additional standards for improving external balance and new forms of consultation and cooperation to that end may be called for.

8. The growing recognition of common interest in the smooth flow of international trade and payments has already greatly promoted the practice of international consultation in the field of finance and trade, which at first tended to be mainly concerned with the fulfillment of, or occasional derogation from, specific obligations, but has more recently developed into a broader cooperation, to ensure so far as possible, that adjustment measures adopted by national authorities take adequate account of the interest of other countries.

9. Much, however, remains to be done in clarifying the measures and instruments which are best adapted to avoiding imbalance and to correcting it as early and as smoothly as possible when it occurs. This is so relevant to the functioning and liquidity needs of the international monetary system that, subject to the review and approval of the Ministers and Governors, we have suggested that Working Party 3 of OECD, which already has gained experience in this field, might be invited to study how member countries, individually and collectively, and compatibly with the pursuit of their essential internal objectives, could in the future preserve a better balance of payments equilibrium and achieve a faster and more effective adjustment of imbalance.

10. Working Party 3 would conduct studies of the interrelationship between internal liquidity and the balance of payments as well as how measures in the field of fiscal, trade, incomes and other policies can be used by both surplus and deficit countries, in combination with monetary policy, to achieve internal and external objectives, par-

ticularly when there is some possibility of conflict between the two. These studies would explore whether standards could be formulated on the contribution of monetary and related policies to balance of payments equilibrium, against which the performance of countries could be appraised. The studies would also cover the relationship of different types of liquidity to the adjustment process, the role of capital movements and capital markets in the adjustment process under conditions of widespread convertibility, and means of improving the process of continuing international consultation and cooperation.

II. Functioning of the Present System

11. The international monetary system is, and doubtless will always be, in a state of evolution, with elements both old and new. Rather than attempt a summary of the whole working of the system as it now is, we set out below the elements which have proved most relevant to the questions referred to us.

12. Gold remains the basic reserve asset of the system and the common measure of par values. But other elements have been added. Much use is made of foreign currencies (particularly the dollar) for intervention by monetary authorities in the exchange markets, as a reserve holding, and in the greatly enlarged international credit facilities now available.

13. The enlargement of the currency element was not the result of any deliberate plan but a gradual process growing out of the spontaneous practices, first of individual traders and bankers, and later of central bankers and national monetary authorities. Under the former gold standard, the maintenance of exchange parities involved passive purchases or sales of gold by central banks in response to initiatives by traders in the markets. But, even under the gold standard, central banks had, on occasion, bought or sold foreign currency to keep the exchange rate away from the gold points. Official intervention in the foreign exchange markets has now become the general practice for keeping the exchange rate within the agreed parity limits. If only for obvious reasons of convenience, intervention is conducted in a currency widely dealt in by traders and bankers throughout the world. Many monetary authorities have seen advantage in accumulating, as a reserve asset, balances of the operating currency which accrue to them in time of surplus.

14. In this way an important supplement to gold has developed in the form of reserve currency holdings (see Appendices I and II). In the decade 1954-63, nearly $6 billion of new gold found its way into official reserves and about $6.5 billion was transferred from the gold holdings of the United States to the reserves of other countries. These additions and transfers were accompanied by an increase of nearly $8 billion in foreign exchange holdings, principally in dollars, during the decade. The practices of individual monetary authorities vary as to the proportion of gold and foreign exchange held in their reserves, but dollars and other foreign exchange accounted for nearly 40 percent of the total reserves of the non-reserve members of our Group (including Switzerland), while the rest of the world held nearly 70 percent of their reserves in the form of foreign exchange.

15. A further distinctive and important feature of the present system lies in the development, since the war, of international monetary cooperation, not only in international organizations, such as the IMF, the OECD, the BIS, and the European Economic Community, but also in smaller or less formal groups. A central role in this cooperation is played by the International Monetary Fund, not only through its large fund of credit but also through its code of obligations. To preserve a framework within which mutual trade and investment can grow freely, member countries undertake to maintain convertibility and stable exchange rates—which does not, however, preclude adjustment to a new stable rate in case of fundamental disequilibrium. The credit element is designed to allow these obligations to be observed, while a country is in deficit, "without resorting to measures destructive of national or international prosperity" (IMF Article I).

16. In view of the importance of the International Monetary Fund in the functioning of the system, it may be useful at this point to recall, in broad outline, its purposes, operating principles and procedures:

(a) As mentioned above, the Fund, under its Articles of Agreement, combines (i) a code of international good behaviour in the field of exchange rates and exchange arrangements and (ii) a central pool of resources available to members, in the form of short- or medium-term loans, in order to help them to observe this code and to shorten the duration and lessen the degree of disequilibrium in international payments.

(b) Each of the 102 member countries has a "quota" determined by reference to such factors as his trade, national income and international payments. Quotas serve three purposes: (i) they determine the amount of the member's subscription; (ii) they measure his borrowing possibilities; (iii) they provide the basis for calculating his voting rights.

(c) Of the quota, 25% is normally subscribed in gold and 75% in the member's currency. Members "draw" from the Fund by purchasing other currencies from it against further payments of their own currency into the Fund. Up to the equivalent of the 25% subscribed in gold (the "gold tranche"), the Fund permits a member to purchase other currencies virtually at will. When transactions flow in the opposite direction and a member's currency is drawn by other members, his position in the Fund improves. If the drawing reduces the Fund's holding of his currency below the original 75% of his quota subscription, his rights to draw virtually at will are *pro tanto* enlarged by what is sometimes called a "super gold tranche" or a "net creditor position in the Fund." Rights to draw from the Fund virtually at will have many of the qualities of a reserve asset; and they are, in fact, so recorded by the Fund itself in its statistics on members' total reserves, as well as by some individual members in their own reserve statements.

(d) A member's drawing rights in his "credit tranches" are normally equal to his quota and can be exercised only in accordance with the Fund's policies. While drawings in the "credit tranches" are subject to stricter requirements as the amount drawn rises, a member may undertake in advance to meet certain conditions laid down by the Fund and so obtain a "standby arrangement" assuring access to the Fund over a limited period of time and for a specified amount. It is the Fund's rule that all drawings be repaid as soon as the drawer's position allows, and, in any event, within a 3- to 5-year period at most.

(e) At any given time, only some of the currencies held by the Fund will be suitable to be drawn. Other currencies will be relatively unsuitable, because the level of reserves of the country concerned is low or because its balance of payments is weak, either temporarily or, as is often the case with less developed countries, for prolonged periods.

(f) Under the General Arrangements to Borrow of 1961-62, our 10 countries have entered into an undertaking to lend the Fund amounts of their currencies up to a total of $6 billion, so as to reinforce the Fund's ability to grant drawings to participants in the Arrangements in order to forestall or cope with an impairment of the international monetary system.

(g) All members' claims on, or liabilities to, the Fund are expressed in terms of a constant gold value as provided by the maintenance-of-value provisions of the Articles of Agreement or of the General Arrangements to Borrow.

17. Since the Fund's creation, its members have drawn a total of $7.5 billion, of which $5.8 billion has been repaid. Drawings have been made by many countries, including among them eight of the members of the Group, three of which have standby arrangements outstanding. In the first 10 years, drawings were made almost exclusively in U.S. dollars with a consequent increase of the super gold tranche rights of the United States. In recent years, however, the balance of payments of the United States being in deficit, drawings have been mainly directed toward other currencies—those of the European countries, Japan and Canada. But repurchases have continued to be made primarily in U.S. dollars, and thus have served to finance part of the U.S. deficit. As a result of these two developments, the U.S. net creditor position ("super gold tranche") of about $1.3 billion which existed at the end of 1958 has largely been replaced by net creditor positions of about $1.1 billion of other members of the Ten. The increased number of countries whose Fund positions have moved into credit during recent years has drawn attention to the fact that, as explained above, countries' gold tranche and creditor positions in the Fund may be regarded as part of their international reserve assets. There are indeed recent examples, besides the United States, in which such a previously accumulated asset in the Fund has been utilized to assist in financing newly-incurred deficits.

18. The sources of credit are not limited to the facilities of the IMF. After the termination of the European Payments Union (and the transition to the European Monetary Agreement), central bank support operations played a more important part, e.g., the Basle ar-

rangements of 1961 and 1963 and the swap and other arrangements established between the United States and other members of the Ten. The Fund's own resources have been enlarged by the 50 percent general increase in quotas in 1959 and reinforced by the General Arrangements to Borrow of 1961-62 which were the origin of the Group of Ten.

19. While our report focuses on official liquidity, private liquidity is also of importance to the international monetary system and to official liquidity. Traders' credits and working balances in foreign exchange are an indispensable part of the day-to-day transactions of private traders and investors; and foreign exchange held by commercial banks as working balances plays a role as a secondary reserve asset along-side official reserves in many national banking systems. Temporary shifts between private and official liquidity can be either equilibrating or disequilibrating but, over time, the probable need for growth of private liquidity should be taken into consideration along with the needs for official resources.

20. Statistical Appendix II shows that, during the decade 1954-63, gold reserves of the Group of Ten and Switzerland rose by about $4¾ billion and their foreign exchange holdings by over $5 billion, while other forms of reserve assets, resulting from transactions with the IMF or from the extension of credits, increased by approximately $2½ billion. These countries as a group also had substantial unused short-term credit facilities in the form of swaps and IMF standbys (about $3½ billion), as well as other short- or medium-term facilities in the IMF.

21. In this connection, it should be noted that credits which monetary authorities extend to one another to finance balance of payments fluctuations normally produce an increase in total gross reserve assets.

22. In sum, a country's liquidity is no longer measured solely by the level of its reserve in the form of gold and reserve currency balances (primary reserves). There is now a variety of ways in which monetary authorities can, at need, replenish their balances of the currencies used for operations. Primary reserves are thus supplemented by a broad spectrum of other resources and facilities (see statistical Appendix II). At one end of this range come "other reserves" of only slightly less liquidity but of unquestioned availability; at the other end of the range are negotiated credits, including

those which will only be available when an international institution is satisfied that the borrower will employ effective adjustment processes to correct his deficit.

III. Appraisal of the Present System and Lines of Future Development

23. The system, as it has evolved up to this point, has shown a great capacity for adapting itself to growth and change, has facilitated the remarkable economic progress achieved since the war, and has withstood with success periods of political and other strain, although many countries are still faced with inflationary pressures and others still have unemployed resources. In these circumstances, it appears to us prudent, 20 years after Bretton Woods, to inquire whether the amount and the character of future liquidity may call for any significant further changes.

24. We find no new considerations which would qualify the view expressed by the Ministers and Governors in their communiqué of 2d October 1963 that "the over-all liquidity of the system seemed fully adequate in present circumstances to cope with possible threats to the stability of the international payments system." Although we know of no satisfactory quantitative formula for the measurement of liquidity needs, we believe that some comments are possible. On the one hand, the fact that some individual countries find themselves short of external liquidity is not *prima facie* evidence of a general shortage of international liquidity. On the other hand, the existence of a general shortage, in its extreme form, might be accompanied by widespread deflationary developments or restrictions on trade and payments resulting from the efforts of governments to defend or restore their reserves. The aggregate needs for liquidity are presumably in some way related to such factors as the growth of world trade and capital movements, and the amplitude and duration of imbalances in international payments, taking into account the efficacy of adjustment policies in correcting such imbalances; they are also affected by psychological attitudes toward minimum or desired levels of national reserves, toward reserve movements, and toward the use of available credit facilities. While there appears to be no convincing evidence that imbalances will be longer-lasting or more intractable than hitherto in the postwar period, a rising turnover of current and capital payments is likely to entail some increase in the size of fluctua-

tions. Moreover, we have noted that a concern for domestic objectives such as growth, employment and price stability, or for international political, monetary and economic responsibilities, may sometimes lead to wider swings in the balance of payments.

25. With regard to the provision of liquidity in the future, the Group has established broad agreement on the following points:

(a) Gold will continue to be the ultimate international reserve asset and common denominator of par values. But, while recent developments lead us to anticipate some continuing increase in world gold production and to expect that the continued success of the gold pool arrangements and other measures will channel a substantial proportion of it into official reserves, we cannot prudently expect new gold production to meet all liquidity needs in the future.

(b) The rise in dollar holdings has contributed somewhat more than monetary gold to the growth of international liquidity in the last decade. The deficit in the U.S. balance of payments now appears to be shrinking and the contribution of dollar holdings to the growth in international liquidity seems unlikely to continue as in the past.

(c) There is no immediate prospect of any other currency assuming the function of an international reserve currency. Indeed, at the present juncture such a development could raise problems without substantially strengthening the system.

(d) The need may in time be felt for some additional kind of international reserve asset. We think it would be timely to investigate the problems raised by the creation and use of such an asset, the possible forms it might take and the institutional aspects associated with it.

(e) Credit facilities—both through the IMF and of a bilateral character—will continue to play an essential part in financing imbalances. Particularly for medium-term credit, the IMF fulfills a valuable and unique function and should continue in its central role.

(f) The recently developed bilateral facilities for swaps and *ad hoc* support operations have already, in periods of stress, been effective in maintaining orderly conditions for international payments in the exchange markets. They should, within a suitable framework for "multilateral surveillance" (see pars. 35-37) continue to play an essential role for short-term purposes.

(g) There is no single, unique manner in which the growing requirements for liquidity have to be met. Past experience shows that, at different times, countries have relied on gold, reserve currencies and credit facilities in different amounts and proportions. Their relative importance may vary from period to period in the evolution of the monetary system, as in the past, but a combination of primary reserves, other reserves, and credit facilities should provide for a needed growth in world liquidity in the future. Viewed from the point of view of the holder, these components of liquidity are, depending on the circumstances, substitutable for one another over a more or less wide margin. In any case, when credits provided by monetary authorities are availed of by the debtor, a form of reserve asset is created in the process.

(h) In view of our increased economic and financial interdependence, the present consultative machinery, whether provided under the IMF, the various bodies of OECD, the BIS, or under other auspices, should be fully utilized by their members and, wherever necessary, provision should be made for closer coordination between the international organizations concerned. The need being to supply sufficient liquidity to finance temporary payments imbalances without frustrating the required processes of international adjustment in individual countries, it is desirable to bring under multilateral review and appraisal the various means of financing surpluses or deficits. Such a "multilateral surveillance," exercised through existing international consultative bodies, would represent a strengthening of the arrangements for international monetary cooperation that have been developed in recent years. This development of a common approach to international monetary matters may well be the main distinguishing feature of the present phase of evolution of the international monetary system.

26. Given the complexity of the problem referred to us, it is not surprising that a number of views were expressed as to the areas which most deserve further study or action for the longer run improvement and strengthening of the international monetary system. Some Deputies considered that it was mainly in the field of the provision of owned reserves under the gold exchange standard that

changes and improvements were desirable. They noted that the present system might imply a reliance on a continuing accumulation of reserve currency holdings, and they stressed the disadvantage of depending for the creation of reserves on the balance of payments deficits of a reserve currency country rather than on the needs of the international monetary system as a whole. Other Deputies stressed the primary desirability of building upon the accomplishments and flexibility of the present system. They noted that reserve currencies were unlikely to make the same contribution as in the past to the growth of international liquidity and believed that principal reliance should be placed on strengthening the international credit component of the present system, and on the increase in reserve assets created when official credits are extended either through the Fund or in some other form.

27. In spite of these differences regarding the best means of meeting adequately the world's future requirements for liquidity, we agreed on the issues of immediate practical concern, and also on the areas in which the development of the international monetary system calls for further study.

28. We have agreed on three main lines of advance: (1) strengthening the international monetary system through the multilateral surveillance of the means of financing both deficits and surpluses; (2) giving support, during the forthcoming quinquennial review of IMF quotas, to an enlargement, by means of a general quota increase, of the credit facilities provided through the International Monetary Fund, and to a relative adjustment of those individual quotas which are clearly out of line; and (3) investigating whether, how, and under what conditions it might be advantageous in the longer run to supplement the existing system by a new type of reserve asset.

29. The practical recommendations on these and other agreed matters, as well as the arrangements for further elaboration on certain questions, are set forth in the remainder of our report.

IV. Conclusions and Recommendations

30. Our recommendations concern:

A—The monetary use of gold

B—Multilateral surveillance of bilateral financing and liquidity creation

C—Further needs for reserve assets

D—International short-term credit facilities
E—Long-term lending
F—The International Monetary Fund

A. *The monetary use of gold*

31. We have reviewed the world situation with respect to gold production and the monetary uses of gold in the light of the statement of the Ministers and Governors quoted at the outset of our report (". . . the underlying structure of the present monetary system—based on fixed exchange rates—and the established price of gold—has proven its value as the foundation for present and future arrangements."). While any projection of the future supplies of monetary gold would be hazardous, we do not believe that the flow of new gold into official reserves can be relied on in fact to meet fully the liquidity needs of the future.

32. In connection with the use of gold for monetary purposes, we have noted with satisfaction the successful coordination, through London, among a number of central banks, of their purchases and sales of gold in the international market. Partly as a result of this there was, during 1963, a marked increase in the flow of gold into official reserves.

33. We consider that leading countries should, according to circumstances, make every practicable effort to discourage speculation in gold and to ensure that as much as possible of the world's new gold supply not required for industrial uses be available to augment official reserves. Full account of this principle should be taken in considering any internal arrangements with respect to gold uses and gold transactions.

34. Moreover, the gold held by monetary authorities should be readily available for use in international settlements, and it is important in this respect that statutory or conventional relationships of gold to the domestic money supply should not prevent gold from playing its proper role in the international monetary sysem.

B. *Multilateral surveillance of bilateral financing and liquidity creation*

35. We have noted that the development in recent years of new techniques—discussed more fully later in our report—for providing

countries with various forms of credit facilities to supplement reserves has brought with it a considerable increase in international monetary cooperaton and better knowledge of the workings of the international payments mechanism. Thus, the central banks participating in reciprocal support operations for meeting short-term payments strains have evolved, through the Bank for International Settlements, facilities for the regular confidential exchange of information and views on such operations. Likewise, various groups within OECD, notably Working Party 3, have provided a forum wherein officials directly concerned with formulation of national policies can review from time to time the balance of payments positions of the various participating countries, the measures taken to adjust imbalances, and the means of financing them. The arrangements put into effect by the International Monetary Fund for consultations with the "Article VIII countries"—that is, those countries with convertible currencies—have also reinforced the fabric of international cooperation.

36. In the course of developing these techniques of consultation and cooperation, the participating countries have been made aware not only of the great gains to be drawn from such an exercise but also of the still remaining shortcomings in their endeavors. Their exchanges of information and the mutually reinforcing actions they have taken have led them to the conclusion that these processes should be continued and intensified. They feel, in particular, that the initiative already taken toward strengthening the multilateral character of the international monetary system should be further developed by bringing within the review and appraisal processes of multilateral surveillance the various elements in international liquidity—whether of a private or official character—available or created for the financing of surpluses and deficits. The object would be to give the monetary authorities of countries participating in the Arrangements a more comprehensive and up-to-date view of major trends and afford them a better basis for strengthening their policy cooperation in the international monetary sphere.

37. We therefore propose that all countries in our Group should provide to the Bank for International Settlements statistical data bearing on the means utilized to finance surpluses or deficits on their external account. These statistical data, combined by the BIS, would be supplied confidentially to all participants and to Working Party 3 of OECD. Any supplementary data would be reported in such detail

and form as the Central Bank Governors may advise. Information would also be exchanged among Central Bank Governors of the Group at the earliest practicable stage on undertakings between members of the Group for new or enlarged credit facilities, with due regard to the recognized need for flexibility in such arrangements. The data and other information would give an indication of trends, leading to a full exchange of views in Working Party 3 of the OECD. This would provide a basis for multilateral surveillance of the various elements of liquidity creation, with a view to avoiding excesses or shortages in the means of financing existing or anticipated surpluses and deficits in the balance of payments, and to discussing measures appropriate for each country in accordance with the general economic outlook.

C. Further needs for reserve assets

38. Taking a longer view, we have discussed various methods of meeting possible future needs for an expansion of reserve assets, apart from new accruals to existing gold and currency balances. A suggestion was made, but not extensively discussed, that the composition of reserves might also be considered in this context, with a view to a gradual harmonization of members' practices.

39. Our discussions mainly concerned two types of proposal: one for the introduction, through an agreement among the member countries of the Group, of a new reserve asset, which would be created according to appraised over-all needs for reserves; and the other based on the acceptance of gold tranche or similar claims on the Fund as a form of international asset, the volume of which could, if necessary, be enlarged to meet an agreed need.

40. Proposals of this kind, which imply a common approach to the process of reserve creation, involve complex questions as to their compatibility with the evolution of the existing system, their merits as a contribution to a greater stability of the international monetary system, their ability to direct liquidity to the point of greatest legitimate need at any given time, their ability to adapt the volume of reserves to global needs as opposed to individual shortages, the acceptability and soundness of the claims they offer as a reserve asset, their effect on relations of the Group with the rest of the world, the machinery required for controlling the volume and distribution of

reserves created, and the desirability of a group approach as opposed
to a worldwide approach.

41. These questions could not be covered in detail in the course
of our meetings and no judgment could be reached on the proposals
until their details had been more fully spelled out and their implications had been further clarified. We have, therefore, established a
Study Group on the Creation of Reserve Assets. This Study Group
would, in appropriate consultation with the IMF and other international bodies, assemble the elements necessary for evaluation of the
various proposals, and report to us as Deputies. It should be clear that
a long-run view is involved and that the decision to embark upon the
study implies no commitment on the part of the participating countries as to its findings.

42. In view of the adequacy of the supplies of gold and reserve
currencies in the present and in the near future, there is no immediate
need to reach a decision as to the introduction of a new type of reserve asset. The studies can therefore be pursued without undue haste.
But, having recognized the uncertainties concerning the future supplies of monetary reserves, we agreed that such studies are timely
and should be put in hand without delay.

D. International short-term credit facilities

43. Official short-term bilateral credit facilities have proved their
value in the working of the international monetary and credit system:

—Swaps and networks of standby swap arrangements are primarily
designed to compensate short-term swings, and, being reciprocal
by nature, are capable of providing mutual benefits.

—*Ad hoc* support operations, such as have been arranged from
time to time in Basle, have similarly been effective in arresting
heavy movements of funds in special circumstances.

These demonstrations of close central bank cooperation are themselves an effective deterrent to speculative movements. Their informal-
ity, speed and flexibility make them especially suitable as a first line—
and short-term—defense against sudden balance of payments pressures. Over the past several years, they have mobilized massive resources in a short time to combat and limit speculative and crisis situations. Their success has greatly reduced the threat to official reserves

from disequilibrating movements of private short-term capital. Such central bank support operations appear to be particularly appropriate to deal with speculative and other movements of funds which are not the outcome of, and do not significantly influence, demand and prices in the countries concerned, and are therefore inherently reversible. While we agreed that the facilities must be sufficiently flexible to supply the funds without delay when needed, we recognize the need for arrangements for exchange of information and review of such operations, as proposed under B, above.

44. We also reviewed the special bonds developed by the United States which are often denominated in the creditor's currency and are redeemable in case of need. Within the consultative framework proposed under B, above, opportunities might be found for discussion on the relationship of this method of financing to other types of credit availabilities, the role of medium-term bonds as a supplementary reserve asset in the portfolio of the lender, and the appropriate maturity for bonds of this nature, as well as possibilities for adapting this type of bond to wider uses among holders.

45. Although we were mainly concerned with credit facilities derived from official sources, we did not overlook certain recent tendencies in the field of private credit. Since the restoration of external convertibility, there has been a general increase in the volume and volatility of private and banking funds. We have no doubt that a growing volume of private credit is indispensable to a further growth in international trade and payments and that action to foster national and international money and capital markets is desirable. Movements of private funds, however, have often been of a disequilibrating kind, requiring policy instruments to be developed and special defenses to be built by international monetary cooperation, to prevent such flows from straining the international monetary system and, if possible, to direct them in an equilibrating direction. A particularly striking development has been the so-called Euro-Currency market, which has helped to channel liquid funds internationally from lenders to borrowers and may at times have had a compensating effect on reserves. On the other hand, too large borrowing of such funds in a situation of basic external deficit may, in taking the strain from the monetary reserves, camouflage the seriousness of a development, offset the self-correcting forces of adjustment and delay deliberate action toward reestablishing external equilibrium.

46. Recourse to foreign short-term credit by commercial banks that takes place under the influence of official action may in certain cases be valuable, but it should not be relied upon generally to reduce the needs for international liquidity available to monetary authorities. In any event, it would be desirable that the members of the Group inform each other, to the extent practicable and within the consultative framework proposed in B, above, as to the scope and character of relevant private movements, especially as they may be influenced by official actions.

E. Long-term lending for monetary purposes

47. While very effective facilities have been developed for short- and medium-term credit between the larger countries, both bilaterally and through the Fund, there has so far been little provision for long-term lending between them for monetary purposes. This reflects the fact that a country that needs credit facilities for overcoming balance of payments difficulties is ordinarily expected—in the interest of international equilibrium and stability—to overcome its difficulties within a reasonably short period of time. It has, however, been suggested by some Deputies that there may be exceptional cases where longer-term lending for monetary purposes between members of the Group might be in the general interest—for example, where a temporary transfer of reserves to the low-reserve country can strengthen it in anticipation of a permanent increase in its reserves to be achieved over a longer period by moderate balance of payments surpluses.

48. There was agreement that no general arrangements for such longer-term lending should be laid down, since this might unjustifiably lessen the pressure for adjustment of existing imbalances. Exceptional cases could therefore be treated on an *ad hoc* basis, after Group appraisal of the concrete case. Some Deputies suggested that, in such cases, it might be useful for a number of countries of the Group to act together on the lending side and, if approved by the Group, there might be some collective understanding that, should a lender subsequently suffer serious reserve losses, others whose reserves were then strong would be prepared to take his holding over, with or without the IMF being associated with the transaction. The consultation and common appraisal within the Group might both lessen the risks and enhance the liquidity of any such lending; at the same time,

it might ensure that the adjustment process between deficit and surplus countries of the Group would not be weakened by such lending.

F. *International Monetary Fund*

49. The quinquennial review of IMF quotas by the Executive Directors of the Fund is due to take place in 1965. The Fund's resources could be enlarged either by a general increase of quotas, in uniform proportions for all members, or by selective increases for some members only, or by some combination of the two, with or without an increase in the General Arrangements to Borrow (GAB). While decisions in this field rest with the competent authorities of the Fund itself, we thought it appropriate, because of the important position of the IMF in the monetary system and because of the special obligations of our countries under the GAB, to explore thoroughly the possible attitude of the members of our Group on the questions regarding the size, timing and manner of providing, if necessary, additional resources to the Fund.

50. The following points were raised during our discussions:

—Adequacy of the Fund's quotas in present and forseeable circumstances.
—The actual use of Fund facilities by members of the Ten and other Fund members in recent years.
—Disparities in size of quota among members.
—Payment in gold of 25% of new subscriptions
—Comparative merits of a general increase in quotas, of selective increases, or of enlargement of the GAB.
—Effect of the above on the liquidity of the Fund.

51. We are all agreed that appropriate credit facilities, particularly through the IMF, provide an element of strength to the international monetary system through financing imbalances while assisting in the process of adjustment. In order, therefore, to provide resources for the Fund in the years ahead, which will no doubt bring a further growth of the world economy, we suggest that the Ministers and Governors of the Group may wish to give their support to an appropriate general increase in quotas during the quinquennial review of the adequacy of Fund resources. We also suggest that there may be some cases in which the quotas of individual members may need to be adjusted on a selective basis.

52. We considered the place of gold in the IMF. Over its whole history, the Fund has had gold receipts of $4.2 billion from subscription payments, repurchases, and charges. The Fund has used $1.1 billion of gold to replenish its holdings of currencies, of which $500 million was used for this purpose in 1961, leaving $3.1 billion. Of this, the Fund has invested $800 milion, the remainder of $2.3 billion being the Fund's present gold holdings.

53. Various functions have been attributed to quota subscriptions in gold:

(a) to provide the Fund with a liquid resource available, if needed, to acquire appropriate currencies necessary for its operations;

(b) to measure the initial amount of drawing rights to which it is the Fund's policy to allow members access virtually at will; and

(c) in some cases, to help moderate any propensity to ask for larger quotas than might be justified.

54. While payments of gold subscriptions to the Fund can reduce a country's gold reserves, its over-all reserve position may be said to remain unchanged if it counts the gold tranche drawing rights which it acquires as part of its reserves. But contributions of gold to the IMF made by nonreserve countries who acquire gold from a reserve currency country can reduce the gold holdings of the reserve center and, in that way, can actually diminish world reserves in the aggregate. In view of these considerations, although we are agreed on maintaining the established principle of payment in gold, attention should be given during the quinquennial review to methods of minimizing the impact, particularly on reserve currency countries, of transfers to the Fund of gold from national reserves.

55. The General Arrangements to Borrow, to which reference has already been made, expire in October, 1966. Any decision on renewal or modification must be taken not later than October, 1965, and will no doubt be related to any increases in IMF quotas, general or selective, that may be agreed. We therefore suggest that a study of this subject should be made over the coming months, in the light of possible action concerning quotas in the Fund, and that a report be made to the Ministers and Governors well in advance of October, 1965.

APPENDIX I

Note: The charts and tables following are selected from those accompanying the original text; Tables I and II have been deleted, Tables III and IV are condensed, but the original numbering of the column headings is retained.—R. V. R.

GOLD AND FOREIGN EXCHANGE HOLDINGS

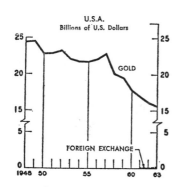

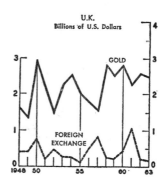

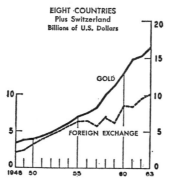

APPENDIX II

TABLE III—OFFICIAL RESERVES AND CREDIT FACILITIES [1]

December 31, 1953-December 31, 1963 [In billions of U.S. dollars equivalent]

	RESERVES				CREDIT FACILITIES				
	GOLD AND FOREIGN EXCHANGE		OTHER		ASSURED	SUBJECT TO NEGOTIATION			
	Gold	Foreign exchange	Sub-total (4) to (7)	Total reserves (3)+(8)	Sub-total (10, 11, 12)	Sub-total (14)+(15)	Total credit facilities (13)+(16)	Total (8)+(17)	Grand total (9)+(17)
	(1)	(2)	(8)	(9)	(13)	(16)	(17)	(18)	(19)
The Eight and Switzerland:									
1953	5.49	5.05	.26	10.80	0	1.48	1.48	1.74	12.28
1963	16.44	10.13	2.70	29.27	1.03	3.74	4.77	7.47	34.04
Change	+10.95	+5.08	+2.44	+18.47	+1.03	+2.26	+3.29	+5.73	+21.76
United Kingdom:									
1953	2.26	.28	.12	2.66	0	1.30	1.30	1.42	3.96
1963	2.48	.17	.49	3.14	1.01	1.44	2.45	2.94	5.59
Change	+.22	—.11	+.37	+.48	+1.01	+.14	+1.15	+1.52	+1.63

United States:									
1953	22.10	0	1.37	23.47	0	2.75	2.75	4.12	26.22
1963	15.60	.21	1.09	16.90	1.58	4.12	5.70	6.79	22.60
Change	−6.50	+.21	−.28	−6.57	+1.58	+1.37	+2.95	+2.67	−3.62
Group of Ten and Switzerland:									
1953	29.85	5.33	1.75	36.93	0	5.53	5.53	7.28	42.46
1963	34.52	10.51	4.28	49.31	3.62	9.30	12.92	17.20	62.23
Change	+4.67	+5.18	+2.53	+12.38	+3.62	+3.77	+7.39	+9.92	+19.77
Rest of World:									
1953	4.47	11.78	.14	16.39	0	1.61	1.61	1.75	18.00
1963	5.68	14.56	.66	20.90	.05	4.18	4.23	4.89	25.13
Change	+1.21	+2.78	+.52	+4.51	+.05	+2.57	+2.62	+3.14	+7.13
All Countries:									
1953	34.32	17.11	1.89	53.32	0	7.14	7.14	9.03	60.46
1963	40.20	25.07	4.94	70.21	3.67	13.48	17.15	22.09	87.36
Change	+5.88	+7.96	+3.05	+16.89	+3.67	+6.34	+10.01	+13.06	+26.90

[1] Data for other reserves and credit facilities are incomplete and partly estimated.

TABLE IV—OFFICIAL RESERVES AND CREDIT FACILITIES [1]

December 31, 1959–December 31, 1963 [In billions of U.S. dollars equivalent]

	RESERVES				CREDIT FACILITIES				
	GOLD AND FOREIGN EXCHANGE		OTHER		ASSURED	SUBJECT TO NEGOTIATION			
	Gold	Foreign exchange	Sub-total (4) to (7)	Total reserves (3)+(8)	Sub-total (10, 11, 12)	Sub-total (14) +(15)	Total credit facilities (13) +(16)	Total (8) +(17)	Grand total (9)+ (17)
	(1)	(2)	(8)	(9)	(13)	(16)	(17)	(18)	(19)
The Eight and Switzerland									
1959	11.27	6.20	.86	18.33	0	3.80	3.80	4.66	22.13
1963	16.44	10.13	2.70	29.27	1.03	3.74	4.77	7.47	34.04
Change	+5.17	+3.93	+1.84	+10.94	+1.03	−.06	+.97	+2.81	+11.91
United Kingdom:									
1959	2.51	.24	.07	2.82	0	1.95	1.95	2.02	4.77
1963	2.48	.17	.49	3.14	1.01	1.44	2.45	2.94	5.59
Change	−.03	−.07	+.42	+.32	+1.01	−.51	+.50	+.92	+.82

United States:									
1959	19.51	0	2.00	21.51	0	4.12	4.12	6.12	25.63
1963	15.60	.21	1.09	16.90	1.58	4.12	5.70	6.79	22.60
Change	−3.91	+.21	−.91	−4.61	+1.58	0	+1.58	+.67	−3.03
Group of Ten and Switzerland:									
1959	33.29	6.44	2.93	42.66	0	9.87	9.87	12.80	52.53
1963	34.52	10.51	4.28	49.31	3.62	9.30	12.92	17.20	62.23
Change	+1.23	+4.07	+1.35	+6.65	+3.62	−.57	+3.05	+4.40	+9.70
Rest of World:									
1959	4.59	12.66	.32	17.57	0	3.03	3.03	3.35	20.60
1963	5.68	14.56	.66	20.90	.05	4.18	4.23	4.89	25.13
Change	+1.09	+1.90	+.34	+3.33	+.05	+1.15	+1.20	+1.54	+4.53
All Countries:									
1959	37.88	19.10	3.25	60.23	0	12.90	12.90	16.15	73.13
1963	40.20	25.07	4.94	70.21	3.67	13.48	17.15	22.09	87.36
Change	+2.32	+5.97	+1.69	+9.98	+3.67	+.58	+4.25	+5.94	+14.23

¹ Data for other reserves and credit facilities are incomplete and partly estimated.

[Selected] Notes to Accompany Tables on Reserves and Credit Facilities

Table Column
No.

1. *Gold.* Figures are published data from *International Financial Statistics.*
2. *Foreign Exchange.* Figures are published in *IFS.*
3. Subtotal of (1) and (2) represents the sum of gold and foreign exchange (primary reserves).
4. *Gold Tranche,* including super gold tranche, is published in *IFS.*
5. *Special U.S. Bonds* represent U.S. Government nonmarketable obligations payable in foreign currencies or in U.S. dollars, with an original maturity of more than one year, and convertible at the option of the holder into short-term Treasury obligations.
6. *Swaps Used by Other Party,* that part of a reciprocal swap arrangement that corresponds to a swing credit drawn upon by the other party, and which therefore becomes an asset of the drawee country.
7. *Miscellaneous* includes, but is not limited to, forward or other availabilities, long-term mobilizable securities and other foreign assets that have been acquired by monetary authorities, such as IBRD notes.
9. *Total Reserves* represent the sum of primary and other reserves. Total may not be statistically exact since some countries treat special U.S. bonds as part of foreign exchange reserves and therefore there may be some element of double counting. This also applies to Columns 8, 18 and 19.
10. *Swaps Unactivated.* This represents the standby facilities that have been established under swap agreements but not activated in the sense of reciprocal acquisition of foreign exchange.
11. *IMF Standbys.* This column would include standby facilities that can be drawn upon without further policy review; there was one of these in existence on December 31, 1963.
16. Includes IMF tranches and any other credit facilities that may be negotiated, or may be available after negotiation under some kind of policy review.

MEMBERS OF THE GROUP OF DEPUTIES

Chairman, ROBERT V. ROOSA. *Vice-Chairman,* JHR. E. VAN LENNEP.

Belgium: M. d'Haeze, Ministry of Finance; C. de Strycker, National Bank of Belgium.

Canada: A. F. W. Plumptre, Ministry of Finance; R. W. Lawson, Bank of Canada.

France: A. de Lattre, Ministry of Finance; B. Clappier, Bank of France.

Federal Republic of Germany: R. Gocht, Federal Ministry of Economic Affairs; O. Emminger, German Bundesbank.

Italy: G. Rota, Ministry of the Treasury; R. Ossola, Bank of Italy.

Japan: Gengo Suzuki, Ministry of Finance; Makoto Watanabe, Ministry of Finance; Haruo Mayekawa, Bank of Japan.

Netherlands: Jhr. E. van Lennep, Ministry of Finance; Prof. S. Posthuma, Netherlands Bank.

Sweden: Krister Wickman, Ministry of Finance; S. F. Joge, Bank of Sweden.

United Kingdom: Sir Denis Rickett, H. M. Treasury; M. H. Parsons, Bank of England.

United States: Robert V. Roosa, Treasury Department; J. Dewey Daane, Federal Reserve System.

Secretaries: Pierre Esteva, Bank of France. G. Schleiminger, German Bundesbank. L. P. Thompson-McCausland, Bank of England. T. de Vries, Netherlands Bank. George H. Willis, U.S. Treasury.

Observers: M. Iklé, National Bank of Switzerland. J. J. Polak, I.M.F. J. Cottier, O.E.C.D. Milton Gilbert, B.I.S.

INDEX

PUBLICATIONS

FOREIGN AFFAIRS (quarterly), edited by Hamilton Fish Armstrong.

THE UNITED STATES IN WORLD AFFAIRS (annual). Volumes for 1931, 1932 and 1933, by Walter Lippmann and William O. Scroggs; for 1934-1935, 1936, 1937, 1938, 1939 and 1940, by Whitney H. Shepardson and William O. Scroggs; for 1945-1947, 1947-1948 and 1948-1949, by John C. Campbell; for 1949, 1950, 1951, 1952, 1953 and 1954, by Richard P. Stebbins; for 1955, by Hollis W. Barber; for 1956, 1957, 1958, 1959, 1960, 1961, 1962 and 1963, by Richard P. Stebbins.

DOCUMENTS ON AMERICAN FOREIGN RELATIONS (annual). Volume for 1952 edited by Clarence W. Baier and Richard P. Stebbins; for 1953 and 1954, edited by Peter V. Curl; for 1955, 1956, 1957, 1958 and 1959, edited by Paul E. Zinner; for 1960, 1961, 1962 and 1963, edited by Richard P. Stebbins.

POLITICAL HANDBOOK AND ATLAS OF THE WORLD (annual), edited by Walter H. Mallory.

AFRICAN BATTLELINE: American Policy Choices in Southern Africa, by Waldemar A. Nielsen (1965).

NATO IN TRANSITION: The Future of the Atlantic Alliance, by Timothy W. Stanley (1965).

ALTERNATIVE TO PARTITION: For a Broader Conception of America's Role in Europe, by Zbigniew Brzezinski (1965).

THE TROUBLED PARTNERSHIP: A Re-Appraisal of the Atlantic Alliance, by Henry A. Kissinger (1965).

REMNANTS OF EMPIRE: The United Nations and the End of Colonialism, by David W. Wainhouse (1965).

THE EUROPEAN COMMUNITY AND AMERICAN TRADE: A Study in Atlantic Economics and Policy, by Randall Hinshaw (1964).

THE FOURTH DIMENSION OF FOREIGN POLICY: Educational and Cultural Affairs, by Philip H. Coombs (1964).

AMERICAN AGENCIES INTERESTED IN INTERNATIONAL AFFAIRS (Fifth Edition), compiled by Donald Wasson (1964).

JAPAN AND THE UNITED STATES IN WORLD TRADE, by Warren S. Hunsberger (1964).

FOREIGN AFFAIRS BIBLIOGRAPHY, 1952-1962, by Henry L. Roberts (1964).

THE DOLLAR IN WORLD AFFAIRS: An Essay in International Financial Policy, by Henry G. Aubrey (1964).

ON DEALING WITH THE COMMUNIST WORLD, by George F. Kennan (1964).

FOREIGN AID AND FOREIGN POLICY, by Edward S. Mason (1964).

THE SCIENTIFIC REVOLUTION AND WORLD POLITICS, by Caryl P. Haskins (1964).

AFRICA: A Foreign Affairs Reader, edited by Philip W. Quigg (1964).

THE PHILIPPINES AND THE UNITED STATES: Problems of Partnership, by George E. Taylor (1964).

SOUTHEAST ASIA IN UNITED STATES POLICY, by Russell H. Fifield (1963).

UNESCO: ASSESSMENT AND PROMISE, by George N. Shuster (1963).

THE PEACEFUL ATOM IN FOREIGN POLICY, by Arnold Kramish (1963).

THE ARABS AND THE WORLD: Nasser's Arab Nationalist Policy, by Charles D. Cremeans (1963).

TOWARD AN ATLANTIC COMMUNITY, by Christian A. Herter (1963).

THE SOVIET UNION, 1922-1962: A Foreign Affairs Reader, edited by Philip E. Mosely (1963).

THE POLITICS OF FOREIGN AID: American Experience in Southeast Asia, by John D. Montgomery (1962).

SPEARHEADS OF DEMOCRACY: Labor in the Developing Countries, by George C. Lodge (1962).

LATIN AMERICA: Diplomacy and Reality, by Adolf A. Berle (1962).

THE ORGANIZATION OF AMERICAN STATES AND THE HEMISPHERE CRISIS, by John C. Dreier (1962).

THE UNITED NATIONS: Structure for Peace, by Ernest A. Gross (1962).

THE LONG POLAR WATCH: Canada and the Defense of North America, by Melvin Conant (1962).

ARMS AND POLITICS IN LATIN AMERICA (Revised Edition), by Edwin Lieuwen (1961).

THE FUTURE OF UNDERDEVELOPED COUNTRIES: Political Implications of Economic Development (Revised Edition), by Eugene Staley (1961).

SPAIN AND DEFENSE OF THE WEST: Ally and Liability, by Arthur P. Whitaker (1961).

SOCIAL CHANGE IN LATIN AMERICA TODAY: Its Implications for United States Policy, by Richard N. Adams, John P. Gillin, Allan R. Holmberg, Oscar Lewis, Richard W. Patch, and Charles W. Wagley (1961).

FOREIGN POLICY: THE NEXT PHASE: The 1960s (Revised Edition), by Thomas K. Finletter (1960).

DEFENSE OF THE MIDDLE EAST: Problems of American Policy (Revised Edition), by John C. Campbell (1960).

COMMUNIST CHINA AND ASIA: Challenge to American Policy, by A. Doak Barnett (1960).

FRANCE, TROUBLED ALLY: De Gaulle's Heritage and Prospects, by Edgar S. Furniss, Jr. (1960).

THE SCHUMAN PLAN: A Study in Economic Cooperation, 1950-1959, by William Diebold, Jr. (1959).

SOVIET ECONOMIC AID: The New Aid and Trade Policy in Underdeveloped Countries, by Joseph S. Berliner. (1958).

RAW MATERIALS: A Study of American Policy, by Percy W. Bidwell (1958).

NATO AND THE FUTURE OF EUROPE, by Ben T. Moore (1958).

AFRICAN ECONOMIC DEVELOPMENT, by William Hance (1958).

INDIA AND AMERICA: A Study of Their Relations, by Phillips Talbot and S. L. Poplai (1958).

NUCLEAR WEAPONS AND FOREIGN POLICY, by Henry A. Kissinger (1957).

MOSCOW-PEKING AXIS: Strength and Strains, by Howard L. Boorman, Alexander Eckstein, Philip E. Mosely and Benjamin Schwartz (1957).

RUSSIA AND AMERICA: Dangers and Prospects, by Henry L. Roberts (1956).